Psychology of Perception

Simon Grondin

Psychology of Perception

 Springer

Simon Grondin
Université Laval
École de Psychologie
Québec, Canada

ISBN 978-3-319-31789-2   ISBN 978-3-319-31791-5   (eBook)
DOI 10.1007/978-3-319-31791-5

Library of Congress Control Number: 2016938797

Printed on acid-free paper

This Springer imprint is published by Springer Nature
The registered company is Springer International Publishing AG Switzerland

Preface

This book is a translation of "Psychologie de la perception" published by the *Presses de l'Université Laval* and has the same name as a course offered at the School of Psychology of Laval University, Québec. It is not a coincidence; the book was written for students of this course. Over the years, whether at Laurentian University a few decades ago or at Laval University since 1996, I learned a lot from the questions and needs for clarification voiced by the students. The book is partly a response to the requested explanations regarding some of the main phenomena, techniques, and principles encountered in the field of perception.

I would like to thank Anne-Marie Grondin who produced numerous illustrations contained in this book; Tsuyoshi Kuroda, expert in psychoacoustics, who provided many tips and some figures in the preparation of Chaps. 2 and 3; and Daniel Voyer of the University of New Brunswick for his fine revision of the content.

Québec, QC, Canada   Simon Grondin

Contents

1 **Psychophysics** 1
   1.1 Detection 1
      1.1.1 Absolute Threshold and Method of Constant Stimuli 2
      1.1.2 Signal Detection Theory 3
   1.2 Discrimination 6
      1.2.1 Difference Threshold and Method of Constant Stimuli 6
      1.2.2 Weber's Law of Discrimination and Its Generalized
            Form 8
   1.3 Other Methods for Estimating Thresholds 9
      1.3.1 The Method of Adjustment 9
      1.3.2 The Method of Limits 10
      1.3.3 Adaptive Methods 12
   1.4 Scaling 13
      1.4.1 Methods 14
      1.4.2 Stevens's Law 14
      1.4.3 Other Contributions from Stevens 15

2 **Physical and Biological Bases of Hearing** 17
   2.1 Physical Characteristics of a Simple Sound Wave 17
      2.1.1 Frequency and Phase 17
      2.1.2 Amplitude 19
   2.2 Physical Characteristics of a Complex Sound Wave 20
   2.3 Subjective Characteristics of Sounds 22
      2.3.1 Pitch, Loudness, and Timbre 23
      2.3.2 Other Subjective Characteristics 24
   2.4 Biological Bases 24
      2.4.1 Outer, Middle, and Inner Ear 25
      2.4.2 The Cochlea 27
      2.4.3 Central Mechanisms 28

      2.5   Theories of Hearing 28
            2.5.1   Frequency Theory 29
            2.5.2   Theories Based on Location...................................... 30
      2.6   Clinical Aspects 32

3   **Hearing**.. 35
      3.1   Perceptual Organization... 35
            3.1.1   Streaming 36
            3.1.2   Illusion of Continuity and Gap Transfer.................. 36
      3.2   Sound Location 39
            3.2.1   Location of Direction... 40
            3.2.2   Location of Distance 41
      3.3   Hearing Music.. 43
            3.3.1   Technical Description 43
            3.3.2   Subjective Experience 45
      3.4   Hearing Speech 46
            3.4.1   Linguistic Description.. 46
            3.4.2   Technical Analysis 48
            3.4.3   Theoretical Perspectives 49
            3.4.4   Intermodality... 51

4   **Biological Bases of Visual Perception**..................................... 53
      4.1   The Eye 53
            4.1.1   The Eyeball 53
            4.1.2   The Retina 55
      4.2   Receptive Fields 57
      4.3   Central Mechanisms... 59
            4.3.1   The Visual Cortex 60
            4.3.2   Visual Pathways 61
      4.4   Clinical Aspects 63

5   **Color Perception** 67
      5.1   Description of Light.. 67
            5.1.1   Intensity... 68
            5.1.2   Wavelength and Spectral Composition 68
      5.2   Perceptual Dimensions of Color 70
      5.3   Color Mixtures 70
            5.3.1   Primary Colors 71
            5.3.2   Addition and Subtraction 72
      5.4   Theories of Color Vision.. 74
      5.5   Chromatic Effects 76
      5.6   Clinical Aspects 80

6   **Form Perception**.. 83
      6.1   Perception of Contours 83
            6.1.1   Edges and Subjective Contours............................... 84
            6.1.2   Lateral Inhibition 85

	6.1.3	Mach Bands	86
	6.1.4	Factors Influencing the Perception of Contours	87
6.2	Gestalt: Perceptual Organization		89
	6.2.1	Figure/Ground Distinction	90
	6.2.2	Perceptual Grouping	92
6.3	Theory of Multiple Spatial Channels		93
	6.3.1	Basic Concepts	93
	6.3.2	Contrast Sensitivity Function	97
6.4	Form Recognition		98
	6.4.1	Templates or Characteristics?	98
	6.4.2	A Computational Approach	99
	6.4.3	A Structural Model	100
	6.4.4	Agnosia	101

7 Depth Perception 103
7.1 Cues for Perceiving a Third Dimension 103
    7.1.1 Binocular Cues 104
    7.1.2 Monocular Cues 106
7.2 Perceptual Constancy 111
    7.2.1 Types of Constancy 111
    7.2.2 Interpretations and Investigations 112
    7.2.3 Gibson's Perspective 114
7.3 Illusions 115
    7.3.1 Variety of Illusions 115
    7.3.2 The Moon Illusion 118

8 Perception and Attention 123
8.1 What Is Attention? 124
    8.1.1 Blindnesses 124
8.2 Preparation and Orientation 125
    8.2.1 Spatial Preparation 125
    8.2.2 Temporal Preparation 127
8.3 Selectivity 128
    8.3.1 Visual Selectivity 128
    8.3.2 Auditory Selectivity 130
8.4 Visual Search 133
8.5 Clinical Aspects 135

Appendix A: ROC Curves 137

Appendix B: Fechner's Law 139

Appendix C: The Nervous System 141

References 147

Index 153

About the Author

Simon Grondin is a Professor at the School of Psychology of Laval University, Québec. His research interests are mainly on timing and time perception, rhythm, psychological time, psychophysics, cognitive neurosciences, and the relative age effect in sports. He is a former editor of the *Canadian Journal of Experimental Psychology* (2006–2009) and a former associate editor of *Attention, Perception and Psychophysics* (2006–2015).

Chapter 1
Psychophysics

A field of psychology, *psychophysics* has as main concern the understanding of the passage of a physical event into a psychological reality. Researchers in psychophysics examine the link between the physical measurement of a stimulation and the psychological measurement of this stimulation. Psychophysicists are primarily interested in three types of capabilities: detecting stimuli, discriminating them, and estimating their value (scaling). The first two types are associated with the fundamental concepts of absolute threshold and differential threshold, respectively.

1.1 Detection

The different sensory systems provide information on the physical and chemical changes that may occur in the environment. A fundamental objective of psychophysics is to assess the minimum amplitude that these changes must have so that an individual can be notified. This minimum amplitude, that is to say the smallest amount of energy that can be detected in the absence of any stimulation, is called *absolute threshold*. Below this threshold, sensation is not possible. However, this threshold is a point whose identification corresponds to an operational definition for a given method. Traditional psychophysics offers several methods for estimating a threshold. The most conventional are the method of constant stimuli, the method of limits, and the method of adjustment. For now, only the constant method is presented:

Gustav Fechner

One could say that psychophysics started in 1860 with the publication of the book *Elements of psychophysics* by the German researcher Gustav Theodor Fechner (1801–1887). Philosopher and physicist, the founder of psychophysics wanted to study the links between the inner world and the outer world. Also known under the pseudonym of "Dr. Mise", Fechner, who worked in Leipzig, had quite a special mind. We owe him various experimental methods still used in psychophysics, but he was also interested in, for example, the properties of the electric current, experimental aesthetics, and even life after death. Note

© Springer International Publishing Switzerland 2016
S. Grondin, *Psychology of Perception*, DOI 10.1007/978-3-319-31791-5_1

that there is an annual meeting of psychophysics, usually held in October, called Fechner Day (October 22). This meeting is held in different locations around the world under the supervision of the International Society for Psychophysics (http://www.ispsychophysics. org/), founded in 1985 in southern France.

1.1.1   Absolute Threshold and Method of Constant Stimuli

For measuring an absolute threshold with the method of constant stimuli, also called the constant method, one must first determine the threshold roughly by locating a region for which a stimulus is almost never perceived and for which a stimulus is almost always perceived. Then, we generally select from five to nine stimuli located between these regions. After this selection, the selected stimuli are presented repeatedly in random order. The method requires an observer to make at least a hundred judgments, but of course, increasing the number of trials for estimating a threshold decreases the risk that the estimated value is far from what the real threshold is.

At each presentation, an observer has to indicate whether or not the stimulus is perceived. It becomes then possible to obtain a discrete (not continuous) frequency distribution, each point representing the number of times a stimulus was detected. These frequencies have to be transformed into probabilities. It is on the basis of these probabilities that the threshold value will be estimated. The probability calculated for each stimulus can be reported on a figure. As shown in Fig. 1.1, the percentage of

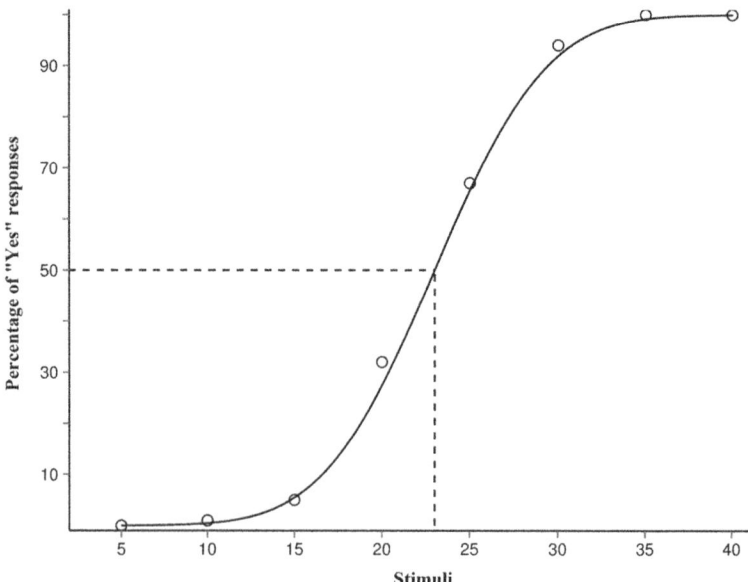

Fig. 1.1 Illustration of a hypothetical psychometric function for absolute threshold. On the *y*-axis is the percentage of times where the observer reports perceiving the stimulus. The *dotted vertical line* reaching the *x*-axis indicates the absolute threshold

times the stimulus is detected is placed on the y-axis and is plotted as a function of the magnitude of the stimuli, placed on the x-axis, in ascending order. The function that relates the probability of detecting to the magnitude of a physical continuum is called a psychometric function. Such a function generally has the shape of an ogive—a kind of S—and the threshold is operationally defined as the point corresponding to an ability to perceive the stimulus 50 % of the time. This value, 50 %, represents the point for which an observer is able to detect the stimulus at a level higher than what would provide responses made randomly in a procedure involving two responses, yes or not.

For drawing a function on the basis of a series of points, it is necessary to posit some assumptions. First, the phenomenon under investigation is assumed to be a continuous random variable. Thus, we shall believe that the discrete distribution obtained (series of points) is an approximation of a continuous function. Also, it is necessary to make an assumption about the shape of this function. Mathematics offers several possibilities, but a function often used in psychology is the normal distribution. The reader is probably already familiar with the concept of normal distribution (normal or Gaussian curve or bell-shaped curve). The function used to draw a psychometric function is derived from the bell-shaped function (probability density function) and is called cumulative normal function. It is after drawing this function that it becomes possible to estimate the threshold value accurately. Besides the cumulative Gaussian function, Weibull and logistics functions are probably the most likely ones to be used (Macmillan & Creelman, 1991).

1.1.2   Signal Detection Theory

Despite the rigor used to estimate the ability to detect a stimulus with the constant stimuli method, a major problem may arise. The estimated capacity may depend not only on the sensitivity of an observer but also on the way in which this observer makes decisions. An observer might as well wait to be sure before making a decision, before declaring that a stimulus is perceived, whereas another observer, in spite of doubt, would tend to say "yes, I perceive" (Macmillan & Creelman, 1991).

There is a method, developed in the 1940s, to determine the sensitivity of the observer to detect a stimulus while correcting the problem associated with the involvement of decision making. Thus, the signal detection theory (SDT), also known as sensory decision theory, uses two parameters to describe the performance: one describing the sensitivity level and the other describing the way an observer makes a decision (Macmillan & Creelman, 1991).

1.1.2.1   Basic Concepts

To understand the SDT, we must first know two fundamental concepts: signal and noise. Signal (S) and noise (N) are the parts of any sensory message. The stimulus that one attempts to detect, called signal, has precise and stable characteristics.

Noise is rather defined as a random variable that is constantly changing. This variable takes different values which are usually assumed to be normally distributed. Noise is a background against which a signal to be detected is sometimes added. This noise includes an external activity (controlled by the experimenter) and internal physiological activity (generated by the nervous system).

In a typical SDT task, an observer must make the following decision about what was presented: was it noise only (N) or noise with the addition of a signal ($S+N$)? For a given amount of noise, the more a signal generates internal activity (the stronger it is), the easier it is to detect it. These two concepts, N and $S+N$, are generally represented with two normal frequency distributions (Fig. 1.2).

An observer subjected to a signal detection task should adopt a decision criterion. This criterion is often measured with the index beta (β). The adoption of a criterion generates four typical conditions (Table 1.1). From these four conditions, two are linked to the presence of the signal and two to its absence. When the signal is present and an observer reports to have perceived it, it is a case of correct identification called a *hit*. When the observer does not detect the presence of a signal when it is presented, we have a case called *miss*. If the signal is not presented but the observer reports that it was, it is a *false alarm*. Finally, not perceiving a signal when actually there was only noise is a condition called *correct rejection*. Table 1.1 summarizes these four typical situations.

Some people prefer waiting to reach some level of certainty before reporting that they have perceived the presence of a signal. These people are referred to as conservative observers, as opposed to lax observers. Two observers may eventually have

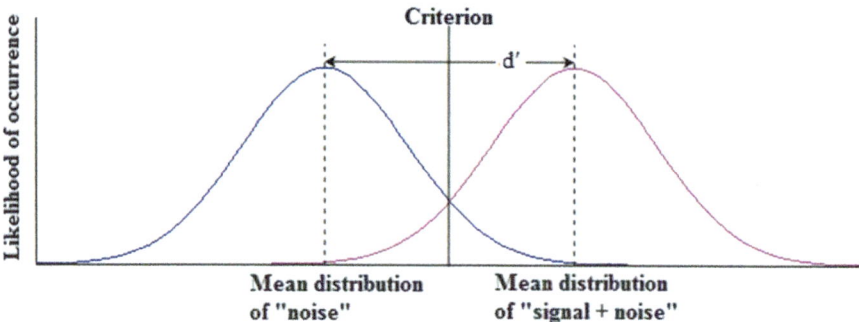

Fig. 1.2 Distributions of noise and signal+noise of the signal detection theory. The *continuous vertical line* represents the criterion. The distance between *dotted lines* represents d', an index of sensitivity

Table 1.1 The four typical situations of the signal detection theory

		Signal	
		Present	Absent
Response	Present (yes)	Hit	False alarm
	Absent (no)	Miss	Correct rejection

similar sensitivities, but adopt different decisional strategies. Compared with a lax observer, the number of hits of a conservative observer might be lower, but the latter would commit fewer false alarms. In short, for a given level of sensitivity, the number of false alarms and the rate of hits may vary, and this is depending on the decisional style of the observer (see Appendix A).

1.1.2.2 Units of Measurement

There are various indices associated with SDT that allow to quantifying the sensitivity of an observer and the criterion adopted. Among the performance indicators used to measure the sensitivity, d' (pronounced d prime) is probably the most common. d' can be defined as the difference between the means of N and $S+N$ distributions, divided by the standard deviation of the noise distribution; d' is a pure index of detectability in that it is not affected by the observer's criterion.

One can easily calculate d' on the basis of hits and false alarms obtained empirically. We obtain an assessment of d' with the transformation into Z-scores of the probabilities of obtaining a hit and a false alarm:

$$d' = Z(\text{Hit}) - Z(\text{False Alarm})$$

For instance, suppose an observer detects correctly the presence of a signal for 90 % of the trials, but commits 25 % of false alarms. Given that the Z-score value for 90 % is 1.28 and the Z-score value for 25 % is −0.67, the sensitivity, d' value, is $1.28 - (-0.67) = 1.95$.

It is important to emphasize that this transformation of percentages into Z-scores is based on the assumption that the N and $S+N$ distributions are normal. Note that there are other performance indices, like Δm or d_e', for estimating sensitivity. Another index, A', is particularly interesting because it allows to estimate sensitivity without having to posit the hypothesis that the distributions are normal. We obtain A', using the following equation:

$$A' = \frac{1}{2} + \frac{\big(p(H) - p(\text{FA})\big) \times \big(1 + p(H) - p(\text{FA})\big)}{\big(4p(H)\big) \times \big(1 - p(\text{FA})\big)}$$

where $p(H)$ is the probability of a hit and $p(\text{FA})$ the probability of a false alarm.

Regarding the criterion, it may be estimated using β. This index is a ratio of the ordinates for each distribution (N and $S+N$) corresponding to the location of the criterion. Thus, the calculation of the β criterion is as follows:

$$\frac{\text{Ordinate of the } S+N \text{ distribution}}{\text{Ordinate of the } N \text{ distribution}}$$

So, in the preceding example, the value of β is 0.552:

Ordinate of 90 % = 0.176 and ordinate of 25 % = 0.319.
Therefore, β = 0.176/0.319 = 0.552.

A high value of β means that the observer is very conservative when making decisions, but conversely, a low β value (<1), as is the case in this example, indicates that the observer tends to be lax. Finally, note that there are also other indicators to express the criterion, including c (Macmillan & Creelman, 1991).

1.2   Discrimination

Another fundamental sensory ability is at play when someone tries to find out if two stimuli are different from each other. The minimum intensity difference required for differentiating two stimuli is called *difference threshold*. As was the case for the absolute threshold, the difference threshold is defined arbitrarily; the threshold value depends on the method used, i.e., on an operational definition. This threshold, the point at which an observer is able to tell the difference between two stimuli, is sometimes called the *just noticeable difference* (JND).

1.2.1   *Difference Threshold and Method of Constant Stimuli*

For estimating a differential threshold with the constant stimuli method, an observer is presented with two stimuli and must determine which of the two stimuli is of greater magnitude. The method includes the presentation on each test of a standard stimulus and of a comparison stimulus. The comparison stimulus usually takes one of seven to nine values distributed around the standard. The standard and one of the comparison stimuli are presented several times, concurrently or sequentially, depending on the nature of the sensory continuum investigated (Grondin, 2008).

In the following example, the purpose is to determine the difference threshold for a standard weight of 250 g with successive presentations of the standard and of a comparison stimulus. The comparison stimulus may take one of the following values: 230, 235, 240, 245, 250, 255, 260, 265, and 270 g. An observer has to indicate on each trial whether the comparison stimulus is lighter or heavier than the standard. After several judgments, it is possible to construct a psychometric function (Fig. 1.3). On the x-axis of the function, the different values of the comparison stimuli are placed in ascending order. On the y-axis, the probability to report that the comparison stimulus is heavier than the standard is reported.

This function enables the identification of two variables that may be important when studying sensation: the *point of subjective equality* (PSE) and the *difference threshold*. The PSE is the point on the x-axis corresponding to 0.50 on the y-axis: the probability to respond that the standard is heavier than the comparison stimulus is the same as the probability to respond that the comparison stimulus is heavier

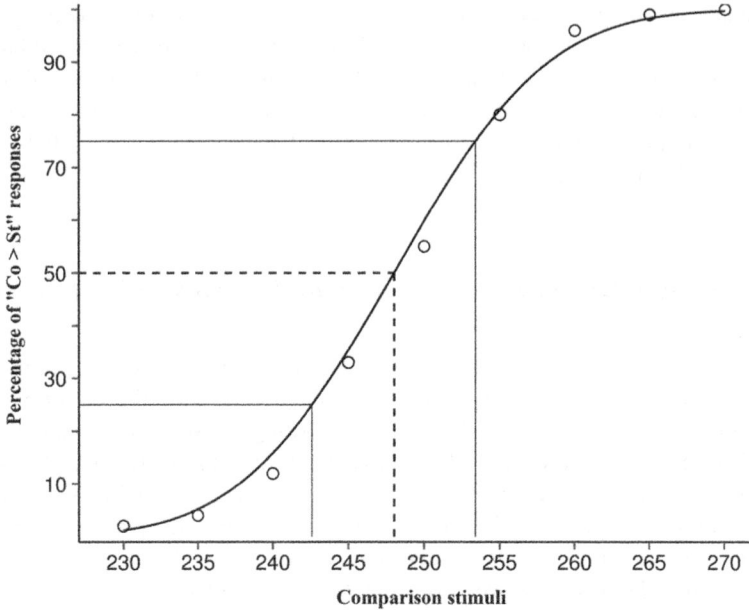

Fig. 1.3 Illustration (hypothetical case) of a psychometric function for difference threshold for weight (standard=250 g). On the *y*-axis is the percentage of times where the observer indicates that the comparison (Co) is heavier than the standard (St). The *vertical and dotted line* indicates the point of subjective equality on the *x*-axis. The other two lines indicate the values that are used for calculating the difference threshold (see text)

than the standard. Furthermore, we call *constant error* the difference between the PSE and the value of the standard.

Two difference thresholds, one above and one below, can be extracted on this function. For the first, we need to subtract the points on the *x*-axis which, on the function, correspond to 0.75 and 0.50 on the *y*-axis. The rationale is the following one: this value, 0.75, is the middle point between a perfect discrimination (100 %) and total inability to discriminate (50 %). In the same way, there is a lower difference threshold: points on the *x*-axis which, on the function, correspond to 0.50 and 0.25 on the *y*-axis. The 0.25 is in the middle of the inability to discriminate (50 %) and a perfect discrimination (0 %). We can obtain a single threshold value by calculating the mean of the two thresholds. It is also possible to calculate directly this difference threshold by subtracting the points on the *x*-axis corresponding to 0.75 and 0.25 on the *y*-axis and then by dividing this value by two.

Finally, it should be noted that classical errors can occur in the determination of difference thresholds with the constant stimuli method. When the stimuli are presented simultaneously, i.e., at the same time, there is a need to vary randomly the side, to the left or to the right, where the standard is presented. This variation seeks to prevent cases where there will be a strong preference for one side or the other. This preference causes what is referred to as the spatial errors. When the stimuli to discriminate are compared sequentially, rather than simultaneously, there may occur a type of bias called a temporal order error. In such a case, the observer will have a more or less marked tendency to judge whether the first or the second stimulus has a greater magnitude. There is often an underestimation of the value of the first stimulus, which could be interpreted as a decrease of the memory trace left by this stimulus (Hellström, 1985).

1.2.2   Weber's Law of Discrimination and Its Generalized Form

There is not only one difference threshold value for a particular sensory modality. In fact, this value varies according to the magnitude of the stimuli used for a given investigation (Grondin, 2001, 2010, 2012). According to Weber's law, sometimes also called the Bouguer-Weber's law (Bonnet, 1986), the difference threshold increases as a function of the intensity of the stimuli being studied. This law states that the minimal magnitude difference, or difference threshold ($\Delta\phi$), necessary to distinguish two stimuli, depends on their magnitude (ϕ). In other words, according to this law, the relationship between $\Delta\phi$ and ϕ is proportional:

$$\Delta\phi = K\phi \ \left(\text{or} \ \Delta\phi \,/\, \phi = K \right)$$

where K, the Weber fraction, is constant. This Weber's law is indeed a principle that provides a tool for looking at the mechanisms involved in the discrimination of sensory quantities in a given sensory modality.

An example will allow grasping fully this relatively simple law. In the previous section, a standard of 250 g was used. If it is known that the difference threshold for a weight of 250 g is 25 g, it can be predicted, on the basis of Weber's law, that the minimal difference to distinguish two weights is 50 g if the standard is 500 g. In other words, the ratio between the difference threshold and the standard will remain the same, 10 % (50/500 or 25/250) in this example.

Although Weber's law may be right for a certain extent of a given sensory continuum, it proves to be incorrect for some values of this continuum. This failure of the strict form of Weber's law has led to a reformulation of the relationship between the difference threshold and the magnitude of the stimulus.

In fact, the Weber fraction is valid only for a limited range on a sensory continuum. For very low or very high values, the Weber fraction is higher. For low values, the increase of the fraction can be easily described based on a transformation of Weber's law. All of what is required is the addition of a constant, a, interpreted as the result of sensory noise:

$$\Delta\phi = K\phi + a$$

Returning to the example above, we can easily understand that for low values, a has a lot of weight in the equation, which is not the case for larger values.

If *a* takes a value of 10, the threshold calculated for a standard, ϕ, of 250 g, is 35 instead of 25, as it would have been the case without the additional noise (*a*). Therefore, the Weber fraction goes from 10 to 14 %. However, for a standard, ϕ, of 2500 g, the calculated threshold is 260 rather than 250. The Weber fraction goes from 10 to 10.4 %.

1.3   Other Methods for Estimating Thresholds

There are many other methods for estimating the value of thresholds, absolute and differential. We describe only two of these below, the method of adjustment and the method of limits.

1.3.1   The Method of Adjustment

With the method of adjustment, the observer has an active participation. On each trial, the observer proceeds to a change. In the case of the determination of the absolute threshold, the observer is presented with a stimulus whose intensity is far below or above the threshold level. The task is to adjust the intensity of the stimulus, either by increasing or decreasing it, so that it is just at the limit of what could be perceived. This method involves a series of ascending and descending trials. It is the average of all observed transition points, between what is perceivable and what is not, which is the estimated value of the absolute threshold. This method is also called the "method of mean errors."

This method of adjustment is not really used to determine an absolute threshold; it is rather useful for the determination of a difference threshold. In the latter case, an observer must adjust a comparison stimulus such that it appears equal to a standard stimulus. To use this method, it is imperative that the stimuli in the study may vary continuously (for estimating both absolute and difference thresholds) and can be presented simultaneously (for difference threshold). The choice of the method of adjustment would not be appropriate, for example, for trying to estimate the difference threshold for auditory intensity. So, after several trials, we can extract two key pieces of information by averaging the points of equality and by calculating the standard deviation of the distribution of points. By subtracting the standard stimulus value from the calculated mean, the constant error is obtained; and the difference threshold will be revealed by the standard deviation. We understand the spirit of this operational definition of the threshold: the greater the standard deviation, the higher the threshold (i.e., poorer discrimination or lower sensitivity). In other words, this means that two stimuli will appear equal over a large range of values.

Consider the following example where two observers, A and B, try to adjust the intensity of a light source to the same level as another source having a fictitious value of 100. The adjustment of each observer at each trial is reported in Table 1.2.

Table 1.2 Adjusted value of the comparison stimulus obtained on each trial with a standard having a value of 100

Observer/trial	1	2	3	4	5	6	7	8	9	10
A	98	99	104	97	102	103	97	102	93	101
B	91	97	89	108	111	99	93	108	95	100

Point of subjective equality of Observer A, 99.6; for Observer B, 99.1
Difference threshold of Observer A, **3.41**; for Observer B, **7.65**

We can see that, on average, there is little difference between them, but we understand that there is much more variability in the scores of Observer B. It is the estimate of this variability that is used to establish the sensitivity level, i.e., the difference threshold.

1.3.2   The Method of Limits

One can just as easily measure an absolute threshold or a difference threshold with the method of limits. In both cases, the method requires the presentation of two types of series of stimuli, one ascending and the other descending. However, in addition to presenting one stimulus at a time (absolute threshold) rather than two (difference threshold), the moment for stopping ascending and descending series depends on the type of threshold under investigation.

Thus, for estimating an absolute threshold specifically, it is necessary to identify in advance a series of stimuli that are more or less close to what is believed to be the threshold. These stimuli are presented one at a time, sometimes in ascending order, sometimes in descending order, alternating from one order to another. In a series of ascending presentations, the first stimulus presented is significantly below the absolute threshold; then the intensity is increased gradually from one trial to another, until the observer reports having perceived the stimulus. Similarly, during a series of descending trials, we first use a stimulus that can be perceived easily, and then the intensity is gradually decreased, until reaching the moment of a transition from a trial where the stimulus is perceived and a trial where it is not. Note that the ascending and descending series do not all begin at the same point (Table 1.3). The purpose of this strategy is to circumvent the problem caused by the possibility of committing the so-called anticipation and habituation errors. To determine the absolute threshold, it is necessary to average the transition points, from not perceived to perceived in the ascending series and from perceived to not perceived in the descending series.

We commit a habituation error when we take the habit of answering "no" during an ascending series or "yes" during a descending series. This type of error will result in the first case in an overestimation of the actual value of the absolute threshold and in the second case in an underestimation. An anticipation error occurs when an observer, knowing that there will be a transition point, passes too quickly from "yes" to "no" (descending series) or from "no" to "yes" (ascending series).

Table 1.3 Determination of an absolute threshold with the method of limits (fictitious values) where the observer indicates whether or not a stimulus is perceived

Intensity/series						
	Ascending	Descending	Ascending	Descending	Ascending	Descending
16				Yes		
14				Yes		Yes
12		Yes		Yes		Yes
10		Yes	Yes	No		Yes
8	Yes	Yes	No		Yes	No
6	No	Yes	No		No	
4	No	No	No		No	
2	No		No		No	
0			No		No	
0					No	
Points of transition	7	5	9	11	7	9

Threshold value: $(7+5+9+11+7+9)/6 = \mathbf{8}$

In the first case, the anticipation error will result in an overestimation of the threshold value compared with the real threshold value and will result in an underestimation in the second case.

In the case of a difference threshold estimated with the method of limits, two stimuli are used, a standard and a comparison stimulus (Table 1.4). These stimuli are presented in pairs, either simultaneously or successively. It is the nature of the evaluated sensory continuum that determines the relevance of the presentation mode. For sound, for example, it is better to present the stimuli successively.

After the presentation of the two stimuli, the observer must determine if this stimulus is smaller or larger than the other or if those stimuli appear to be equal. Comparison stimuli vary from one trial to another so that the difficulty of discriminating is gradually increased. If it is an ascending series, the magnitude of the comparison stimuli is increased; for a descending series, the magnitude is decreased.

Determining the difference threshold with the method of limits, instead of the absolute threshold, is particular for not having a series, either ascending or descending, being stopped when a transition point is observed. In fact, in the case of an ascending series, for example, the first transition that the observer meets is when the comparison stimulus appears to be smaller than the standard and then, the following trial, the stimuli appear equal. It is necessary to continue to increase the value of the comparison stimuli until the standard and comparison stimuli stop appearing equal. It is necessary to reach the transition that leads to the impression that the comparison stimulus is larger than the standard. Once this response is made for the first time, the series ends (Table 1.4). The same process is followed with the descending series. Also, just as was the case for the absolute threshold, ascending and descending series have to be alternated, and the starting value of a series should also vary from one time to another, for the ascending and for the descending series.

Table 1.4 The difference threshold with the method of limits is based on conditions where the observer indicates that a comparison stimulus is lesser (L) or greater (G) than a standard (of 10, fictitious values) or of equal (E) value

Intensity/series						
	Ascending	Descending	Ascending	Descending	Ascending	Descending
18				G		
17				G		G
16		G		G		G
15		G	G	E		G
14	G	G	E	E	G	E
13	E	G	E	E	E	E
12	E	E	E	E	E	E
11	E	E	E	E	E	E
10	E	E	E	E	E	E
9	E	E	E	L	L	E
8	E	E	L		L	L
7	L	L	L		L	
6	L		L			
5	L		L			
4	L		L			
3			L			
2			L			
Upper limit	13.5	12.5	14.5	15.5	13.5	14.5 ($M=14$)
Lower limit	7.5	7.5	8.5	9.5	9.5	8.5 ($M=8.5$)

Point of subjective equality: $(14+8.5)/2 = 11.25$
Uncertainty interval: $14-8.5 = 5.5$
Difference threshold: $5.5/2 = \mathbf{2.75}$

For each series, there are therefore two transition points. These points make it possible to identify an upper limit (uL) and a lower limit (lL). For example, in the case of a descending series, the uL is reached when, after the comparison stimulus was perceived as being greater than the standard, these stimuli are now perceived as equal. Similarly, the lL is reached when, after being perceived as being equal to the standard during a trial or several trials, the comparison stimulus is now perceived as being lesser than the standard. An uncertainty interval can be calculated by subtracting the average of uL from the average of lL; the difference threshold is then calculated by dividing this uncertainty interval by 2. A PSE is estimated as follows: (uL+lL)/2.

1.3.3 Adaptive Methods

Although we will only touch on the subject, it should be noted that there are a series of so-called adaptive procedures for estimating thresholds. In general, these methods allow to make good estimates of thresholds in a lesser number of trials, in particular by reducing the number of trials involving stimulus values that are far from the threshold.

One of these procedures is the staircase method (Bonnet, 1986). For using it, it is necessary to choose a starting level (more or less close to the threshold) and a step value allowing to change the difficulty level, by decreasing or increasing the magnitude of the stimulus, depending on whether there is a change from "I do not perceive" to "I perceive" or from "I perceive" to "I do not perceive." It is also necessary to decide whether or not the magnitude should be changed as soon as a response indicates the transition from one state to another. Finally, it is also necessary to decide when to stop the procedure, for example, after a number of state changes or after a fixed number of trials. With the staircase procedure, one can use a single staircase having only one set of variations, a double staircase involving two independent series, a series starting well above the threshold, and the other way below.

Another well-known adaptive method is called *parameter estimation by sequential testing* (PEST). Generally, with this procedure, at every reversal in the opposite direction, the step value adopted at the beginning is halved. Also, this step remains the same when there is a change in the same direction or may even increase (be doubled) if, for example, the observer provides a response in the same direction in three consecutive trials (Macmillan & Creelman, 1991). Finally, note that there are other adaptive methods such as those based on a Bayesian procedure or maximum likelihood (Shen, 2013; Shen & Richards, 2012).

1.4   Scaling

A third fundamental question in the field of psychophysics is that of the relationship between the magnitude of a physical stimulus and its psychological magnitude. Such a question is significantly different from that which arose in the context of Weber's law that relates two physical quantities. The questioning is along the line started by Fechner who proposed, using an indirect method, that the relationship between the magnitude of a physical stimulus and the psychological magnitude would necessarily be logarithmic (Appendix B).

For conducting an empirical verification of a law on the relationship between physical quantities, for a given sensory continuum, and the sensory experience that is made, we first have to try to quantify this experience. Stanley Smith Stevens proposes to adopt different methods to measure the experience as directly as possible:

> The American Stanley Smith Stevens (1906–1973) is a prominent figure in psychophysics. He obtained a PhD from Harvard University, where he worked for many years. He is of course well known for Stevens's law and for the development of methods for studying the link between the magnitude of a physical stimulus and its psychological magnitude. What is less known is his contribution extending to other fields, particularly in the field of hearing. We owe him in particular the identification of different measurement scales.

1.4.1 Methods

The empirical demonstrations of Stevens rely on several scaling methods. Essentially, we can distinguish the "partition scale" and "ratio scale."

Among the partition scales, there are category scales and equisection scales. In the first case, an observer must assign each stimulus a set of stimuli in certain categories (for instance, from 1 to 5). The number of stimuli in the set and the number of categories are determined in advance. As for the equisection scales, an observer must divide his psychological continuum into a series of distances considered as equal. For example, the observer may need to determine that the distance between the sensations created by stimuli A and B on a sensory continuum is smaller than, equal to, or greater than the distance between the sensations produced between stimuli C and D, also on this continuum. Among the method-specific equisection scales, there is bisection. In such a case, the observer is required to select a stimulus whose intensity is located halfway between the intensities of two other stimuli.

As for the ratio scales, there are the estimation tasks and the production tasks. A procedure often used is called "magnitude estimation." When this procedure is used, an observer is exposed to a standard stimulus, also called *modulus*, which is assigned a numerical value. Then, at each presentation of a stimulus, the observer must assign to this stimulus a numerical value relative to the standard. The observer sets his own scale around the value of the modulus, taking care of never choosing zero. If a stimulus appears to be twice as intense (greater) than a modulus of 50, the observer will assign it a value of 100. Thus, it becomes possible to establish a correspondence between the different assigned values (psychological magnitude on the y-axis) and the magnitude of the physical stimuli (on the x-axis).

The ratio production (or fractionation) is among the various types of other ratio scales. For example, an observer may be required to produce the intensity of a stimulus such that it corresponds to a percentage (e.g., half or one-third) of another stimulus.

1.4.2 Stevens's Law

Thus, another fundamental question in psychophysics is related to identification and quantification of the relationship between the magnitude of sensation and the physical magnitude of a stimulus. This relationship is sometimes referred to as *psychophysical law*.

Of course, it is reasonable to expect that the relationship between the magnitude of sensation and the physical magnitude of a stimulus will be monotonic, that is to say, that the psychological magnitude increases continuously with the increase of the physical magnitude. The question remains concerning the exact nature of this increase: is it fast at the beginning, for stimuli with low amplitude, and slower when the stimuli are of greater magnitude?

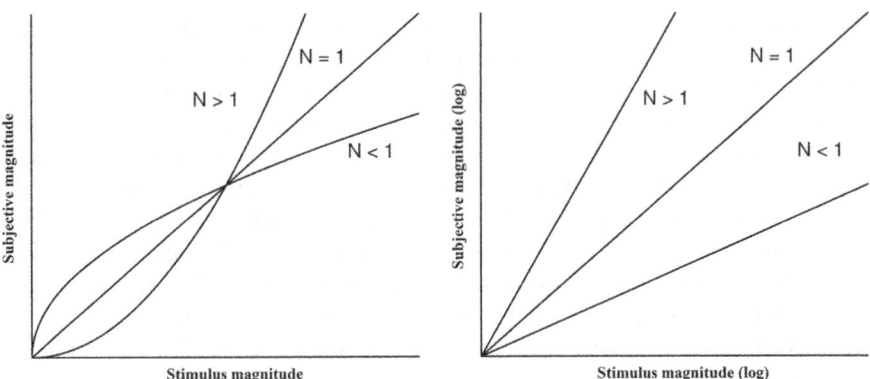

Fig. 1.4 Three types of relationship, exponential $(N>1)$, linear $(N=1)$, and logarithmic $(N<1)$, between sensation and the physical magnitude of a stimulus. *Left panel*: $S = K\phi^N$. *Right panel* shows the same function in log-log coordinates: $\log(S) = N\log\phi + \log K$

In fact, this increase depends on the nature of the stimulus under study. Essentially, as shown in Fig. 1.4 and as reported by Stevens following a very large number of empirical studies, there are three types of growth: exponential, linear, and logarithmic. Thus, Stevens established that the best description of the relationship between the magnitude of perceived sensation and intensity of a stimulus is expressed using a power function:

$$S = K\phi^N$$

where S is the sensation, K is a constant whose value depends on the measurement units used, and N is the exponent specific to a given sensory dimension. This law is called the power law, Stevens's law, and sometimes Stevens's power law.

The exponent N is the main feature of this equation, the signature of a sensory continuum. Its value is 1 if the relationship is linear, is smaller than 1 if the relationship is logarithmic, and is greater than 1 if the relationship is exponential. The N values reported by Stevens (1961) are, for example, 0.55 for smell, 0.60 for loudness, 1.00 for temperature, and 3.50 for electric shocks. These values however are likely to fluctuate from one experience to another. For example, Stevens (1961) reports a N value of 1.0 for the duration, but after a lengthy review of the literature on the issue, Eisler (1976) came to the conclusion that 0.90 is probably a better approximation (see Grondin & Laflamme, 2015).

1.4.3   Other Contributions from Stevens

Stevens (1975) makes a fundamental distinction between two types of sensory experiences. These experiences are part of one of two sensory continua, called *prothetic* and *metathetic*. In the case of a prothetic continuum, the sensory experiences are based on an additive physiological process, i.e., a process in which the increase in the physical intensity of a stimulus leads to an increase of the frequency of action potentials by neurons responsible for receiving these stimuli. In contrast, a metathetic continuum is not based on the idea of addition, but rather on that of substitution.

Thus, with a prothetic continuum, it is logical to try to answer a question based on the idea of "how much?" whereas with the second type, the metathetic continuum, the question rather consists of knowing "of what kind?" the sensation is. For example, in the visual modality, a brightness change will be additive; a light source will be more or less intense than another. Therefore, we will be dealing with a prothetic continuum. If we are dealing with a change in the wavelength of light, the change will be a substitution, that is to say that what will be observed will not depend on a quantitative sensory difference, but on a simple qualitative change in appearance, namely, a change of color (hue).

As mentioned above, Stevens is also responsible for identifying the various measurement scales. He had identified four: the nominal scale, which only serves to identify an object; the ordinal scale, which indicates the rank or order of scores; the interval scale, which includes the notion of distance between the scores; and the ratio scale, which includes, in addition to the notion of distance, an absolute zero.

That said, it is not possible to use the same scale for all the sensory qualities. Some of these qualities can be quantified (prothetic continuum), others not (metathetic continuum). In the first case, the scores can be distributed on an ordinal or even interval scale, but with a metathetic continuum, the nominal scale is appropriate.

Chapter 2
Physical and Biological Bases of Hearing

Hearing relates to the sense responsible for translating a series of pressure variations in the air into an action potential, i.e., something that the brain can recognize. Before describing the biological bases of hearing, it is first necessary to understand what the brain needs to recognize.

2.1 Physical Characteristics of a Simple Sound Wave

Sounds are produced because something vibrates in the environment. These vibrations are disturbances and their propagation is possible only because it happens in a material medium. This medium is usually air, but it could also be, for example, water or any other substance. If you are underwater and try to talk to someone, you will find that this is possible, but the carried message is far from being as clear as it is usually. In short, a body which vibrates produces sound, provided that the vibrations do not occur in a vacuum where nothing is transmitted.

More specifically, the vibrations cause a series of compressions and rarefactions of the molecules in the environment. The normal pressure in the air is successively increased or decreased. As discussed below, the characteristics of these variations can be represented using a simple sine wave (for pure sound).

2.1.1 Frequency and Phase

A key thing to consider in the analysis of sound is the speed of variations ranging from compressions to rarefactions to compressions and so on. These changes occur more or less rapidly. This speed of state changes is called the frequency, i.e., the number of cycles ("compression-rarefaction") completed during a given period. It

© Springer International Publishing Switzerland 2016

S. Grondin, *Psychology of Perception*, DOI 10.1007/978-3-319-31791-5_2

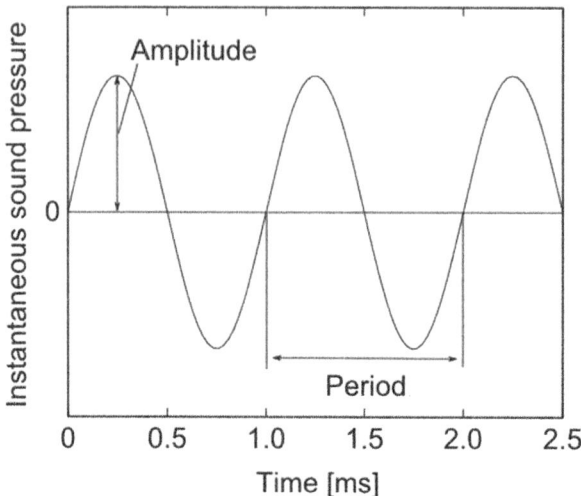

Fig. 2.1 Illustration of a sound (sinusoidal) wave for a pure tone of 1000 Hz (or 1 kHz)

was agreed to express this frequency in a number of cycles completed in 1 s. One cycle per second is 1 hertz (Hz), the unit used to express frequency and named after the German physicist Heinrich Hertz.

The time taken to complete one cycle of the sine wave is called the period (Fig. 2.1). As for the circular motion, a period (or a complete cycle) involves 360° (360 degrees). The beginning of the cycle is 0°, whereas the maximum compression and the maximum rarefaction occur at 90° and 270°, respectively. Also, the relative position of two sounds over time is called phase. If two pure tones arrive at a given point in time with a difference of 1/8 of a cycle, they will be described as being 45° out of phase.

If a sound has a frequency of 1 Hz when a cycle is completed in 1 s, a sound completing 500 cycles in 1 s has a 500-Hz frequency. If a cycle takes only 1 ms to be completed, that is to say, 1000 cycles are completed in a second, it will be a 1000-Hz, or 1-kHz, sound (pronounce kHz "kilohertz").

Sometimes, to express the idea of frequency, we use the notion of wavelength. This is denoted by the Greek letter lambda (λ) and consists of the linear distance between two successive compressions. Of course, the fewer cycles traveled in a given time, the longer the wave. However, this length is also determined by the propagation speed of the wave. Determined by the environment in which the wave is generated, the speed is greater in a denser medium. The speed is, for example, 340 m/s in the air and 1500 m/s in water. Thus, two waves having the same frequency in the air and water do not have the same length.

The span of audible frequencies by the human ear ranges from about 20 Hz to 20 kHz. In fact, toward the ends of this range, the detection threshold is much higher; in other words, to be heard, a sound of 20 Hz must be much louder than a 5000-Hz sound. Also, most often, conversations remain in a range of frequencies extending from about 100 Hz to 10 kHz. Note also that the hearing abilities vary with age; thus, it becomes difficult with age to hear sounds above 15 kHz. In fact, some people, even young people, are unable to hear such sounds. Humans therefore can deal with a wide range of audible frequencies. However, this capability of hearing high frequencies does not compare at all to that of, for instance, mice (up to 90 kHz), bats (over 100 kHz), or dolphins (up to 200 kHz), which are therefore able to hear ultrasounds. In the next chapter (Fig. 3.6), you will return to this notion of frequency ranges emphasizing the ones covered by some musical instruments and by the human voices. Note that the animals who are able to hear ultrasounds will be unable to hear, for example, frequencies below 1000 Hz in the case of mice or 3000 Hz in the case of bats. Elephants, however, hear low-frequency sounds (up to 17 Hz), but cannot hear sounds above 10 kHz.

2.1.2 Amplitude

A second physical characteristic for describing sounds is called amplitude or intensity (Fig. 2.2). This feature refers to the fact that pressure variations may be more or less pronounced. It was agreed to express this magnitude with a unit called the decibel (dB—the name "bel" given in honor of Alexander Graham Bell). Indeed, this unit is issued from a pressure ratio between that exerted by a given sound and that exerted by a reference sound. In such a case, we refer more specifically to dB SPL (SPL for *sound pressure level*).

A pressure measurement is expressed in terms of force per unit of area. Thus, the sound pressure used as a reference is, by convention, 0.0002 dyne/cm^2, a "dyne" corresponding to the force required to give a mass of 1 g an acceleration of 1 cm/s^2. It is also possible to express the pressure with a unit called pascal (named after the scientist and philosopher Blaise Pascal), the reference sound being equal to 20 µPa (micropascal).

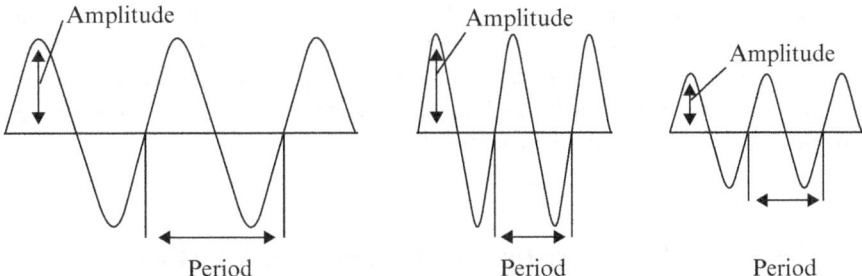

Fig. 2.2 While the wave of the *left* and the one in the *center* have the same amplitude but different frequencies, the wave in the *center* and the one on the *right* have the same frequency but different magnitudes

More specifically, to avoid having to deal with very high numbers, it was agreed to express amplitude as a logarithmic scale. Thus, the number, N, of decibels produced by a sound can be calculated as follows:

$$N\,dB = 20\,\log \frac{\text{Pr}_{\text{sound}}}{\text{Pr}_{\text{ref}}}$$

where Pr_{sound} is the sound pressure that is being measured and Pr_{ref} is the pressure of the reference sound (20 µPa). So, we can easily calculate the amplitude of a sound in dB once we know the pressure this sound exerts. Thus, if a sound creates a pressure that is 100,000 times greater than that of the reference sound, its amplitude is 20 times the log of 100,000, that is to say, $20 \times \log (10^5)$. The log of 10^5 is equal to 5. Accordingly, the sound has an amplitude of "100 dB" (20×5).

The constant "20" used in the calculation of the number of dB is due indeed to two constants: multiplied by 2 and multiplied by 10. The 10 stands for the decision made to use decibels rather than bels; this avoids having to work with decimals. The source of the 2 is a bit more subtle. The bel is indeed a measure of power and not a measure of pressure. Since it is agreed to express the amplitude of sound in terms of pressure ratio, it is necessary to consider what the relationship between power and pressure is. The acoustic power (Po) is equivalent to the acoustic pressure (Pr) squared:

$$Pu = Pr^2 = 2\,\log (Pr),\text{ which explains where the 2 comes from.}$$

In order to have some idea of what some sound intensities represent, here are some examples drawn from everyday life. A simple whisper or rustling leaves reaches a loudness of about 20 dB. A library is never really completely silent, and ambient sound may approach 40 dB, which is still well below the 60–70 dB observed in a work office. In fact, the intensity level of normal speech is around 60 dB. A heavy car traffic creates an amplitude level of about 80 dB, a level that reaches up to about 90 dB with the presence of a large truck or even up to 100 dB with some motorbikes. This remains a little weaker than the 100 dB of a jackhammer or 110 dB (and even more) of certain night clubs, at least near to one of the sound sources. You will understand why workers taking care of the luggage near a large airplane wear helmets to cover their ears, now that you know that large airplanes produce sound intensities of more than 130 dB, which might cause pain. Noises provoked by firing a gun or a pistol can reach more than 160 dB.

2.2 Physical Characteristics of a Complex Sound Wave

Usually, the waves heard in the environment are not pure tones like those described early in the previous section. Pure tones can be created easily in a laboratory, with a tuning fork or with some electronic instruments. Most often, what is heard, whether it is noise, voice, or musical instruments, are complex sounds. While pure tones consist of only a single frequency, complex sounds result from the mixing of two or more waves of different frequencies.

Complex sounds can be periodic or aperiodic. They are periodic when their components are integer multiples of the lowest frequency. The lowest frequency in a sound is called the fundamental frequency (often abbreviated as F0). It is also called the first harmonic. A periodic sound is said harmonic when it contains all the other harmonics. The vowels produced by the voice and the sounds of musical instruments, except percussion, belong in this category (harmonic sounds). If one or a few of these frequencies are missing, the sound is referred to as inharmonic. If a sound is composed of different frequencies that are not multiples of the fundamental frequency, then it is an aperiodic sound. Partials, rather than harmonics, are used to describe the composition of an aperiodic sound.

Thus, the fundamental frequency is the lowest note generated by something vibrating. All the frequencies generated are specific to the properties of what is vibrating. What distinguishes one sound from another is not only the frequency and amplitude, as seen above. The distinction may also depend on what might be called the complexity, i.e., the harmonic series that the sound contains, including its fundamental frequency. Why two sounds having the same fundamental frequency and the same intensity would sound differently is because they have different harmonics.

For understanding the nuances about the complexity of sounds, one approach consists of asking the following question: why do two "Cs" on the piano are "C"? There are two elements of response to this question. On the one hand, two pure tones separated by an octave seem identical. This quality is called chroma. On the other hand, these two "Cs" share harmonics that are not shared by other notes. A 32.70-Hz C and a 65.41-Hz C will both have in their harmonics a C of 130.81 Hz; there exists such a pattern for any other note (D, F, ...). Note, however, that a C of 32.70 Hz has in its harmonics a frequency of 65.41 Hz, but the latter C (65.41) does not comprise the C of 32.70 Hz, the lowest frequency of 65.41-Hz C being actually 65.41 Hz.

Equally crucial is this second question: why, since it has the same fundamental and the same harmonics, does a C of 32.70 Hz sound differently when played on a piano rather than on a guitar? These same "Cs" differ because the relative importance of each harmonic is not the same for both instruments. The relative contributions of each harmonic depend on the vibrating properties of the instruments. The use of an oscilloscope allows to seeing that both identical "Cs" played sometimes on guitar, sometimes on the piano, have a same frequency, but the wave drawn is not the same for each instrument. In each case, however, the configuration is more complicated than that of a pure tone (simple sine wave).

There is a way to know the relative importance of the harmonics of a complex periodic sound. This could be done with a Fourier analysis, named after Jean Fourier, a French physicist of the early nineteenth century. Such an analysis allows describing quantitatively any complex wave into a series of simple components (sine waves). It is interesting to note, as stipulated by the acoustic law of Ohm, that the ear can somehow act as a Fourier analyzer. Thus, if a few notes are played together, the auditory system can extract and hear each of the simple sounds contained in the complex sound that was produced.

White noises enter in the category of aperiodic complex sounds. These sounds are made of the mixture of all frequencies. This name, white noise, is given by analogy to white light which means, as it will be discussed in Chap. 5, not the absence of wavelengths that would allow to observe a color, but the presence of all wavelengths. White noise gives a sound similar to the one we sometimes hear when trying to tune a frequency on a radio, moving through different frequencies without being able to capture a station correctly.

It is possible to create sounds by using a filter that let pass only frequencies included within a certain range. This range is called bandwidth and can be more or less narrow. One can also use high-pass filters that allow the passage of frequencies above a certain value or low-pass filters that allow the passage of frequencies below a certain value.

Another phenomenon, called masking, refers to the incapacity to hear a sound normally audible because of the presence, simultaneously or nearly, of another sound (mask). For example, if two sounds are presented simultaneously, it is possible that both are heard. In some circumstances, i.e., according to their relative frequency and intensity, it is possible that a sound be heard and the other not. Most often, a loud sound will mask a weaker sound; also, a sound will mask sounds of equal frequencies or of higher frequencies. The frequency range that may be masked by a given sound is called the critical band. The mask does not need to be presented simultaneously to exert its influence. It can be shifted in time, but its influence will be greater if it is presented shortly before rather than shortly after the sound that is to be masked.

It should be noted that when a pure tone is produced in a laboratory, this sound may not be clear at the beginning (onset) and end (offset). In order to ensure that the transitions are not too steep, a gradual rise of intensity to reach the targeted intensity, and a gradual fall at the end of the sound, may be used. This shaping of a sound is called the envelope. The sound will be softened even with a rise and fall lasting only a few milliseconds each. Furthermore, if the sound is presented to each ear, we speak of a binaural presentation, as opposed to a monaural presentation if the sound is sent only to one ear.

2.3 Subjective Characteristics of Sounds

The impressions left by the sounds, especially when emitted by human voices or music instruments, are numerous and diverse. But before evoking their potential emotional connotation, it is first relevant to distinguish the broad categories of psychological impressions produced by the sounds that could be linked quite directly to the physical reality.

2.3.1 Pitch, Loudness, and Timbre

One of the subjective characteristics closely related to a physical characteristic is pitch (Hartmann, 1996; Yost, 2009). Pitch refers to the impression that the sound seems low or high. While high-pitch sounds are composed of high frequencies, the low-pitch sounds are made of low frequencies. Therefore, there is a close and direct correspondence between pitch and frequency. However, the pitch is not perfectly correlated with frequency. The intensity, for example, may exert some influence on the pitch.

It is difficult to measure directly a subjective dimension such as pitch. S. S. Stevens (see Chap. 1) addressed this problem based on the responses of observers and working on a new unit of measurement, operationally defined. Stevens thus developed the concept of mel, 1000 mels corresponding to the pitch of a 1000-Hz sound at 40 dB SPL.

A second fundamental subjective dimension of auditory perception is called loudness. This quality mainly refers to the sound intensity, that is to say, the impression that sound seems to be soft or loud. Of course, a high-amplitude sound appears louder than a sound of low amplitude, but this impression may vary depending on the frequency of the sound heard. Just as he developed the mel, Stevens also developed a unit of loudness, the sone, which is the loudness of a 1000-Hz sound at 40 dB SPL.

The fact that loudness depends not only on the intensity of sounds but also on the frequency has been highlighted by many psychophysical experiments that have led to the development of *equal-loudness contours*. These lines, called *phons* and reported in Fig. 2.3, are built on the basis of a 1-kHz standard sound. If the frequencies would exert no influence on loudness, the lines would remain flat. What the figure reveals is the fact, for example, that the loudness of a sound of 200 Hz and 60 dB SPL will be the same (about 50 sones) to that of a 2-kHz sound at 50 dB SPL. Note in conclusion that the impression of loudness is also dependent on the

Fig. 2.3 Equal-loudness contours, each expressed as phons (Fletcher & Munson, 1933)

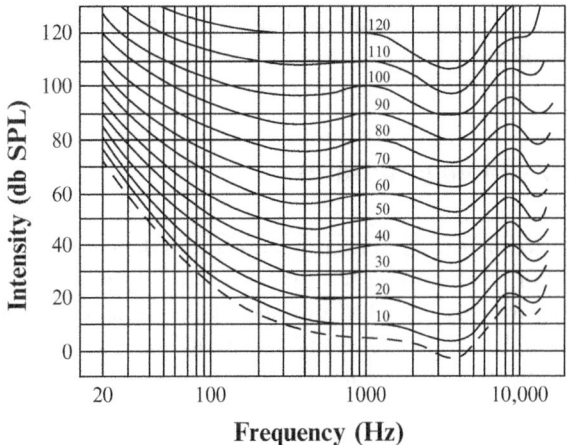

presentation duration of the sound: with very short sounds (<200 ms), the intensity needs to be increased for generating the impression that this sound is as loud as a sound of longer duration.

A third subjective dimension of the auditory experience closely related to physical reality is called timbre. As reported above, two sounds may have the same fundamental frequency and the same amplitude, but they may nevertheless be different perceptually. What causes this difference is their timbre, which depends on the composition of each sound, i.e., on their respective harmonic arrangements.

2.3.2   *Other Subjective Characteristics*

Sounds can create many other subjective impressions. For example, we will have the impression that space is more or less filled by a sound. In such a case, we refer to volume (not to be confused with intensity). Of course, if we increase the intensity, the impression of volume is increased; the volume also appears greater if the pitch of a sound is low rather than high. Another subjective impression is related to the fact that a sound may seem more or less compact, or more or less hard. This quality of a sound is referred to as density, a loud sound dominated by high frequencies appearing denser than a weaker sound dominated by low frequencies.

In fact, the subjective impression caused by a sound can often be associated with its spectral composition. Already in the nineteenth century, Helmholtz reported that a sound composed only of its fundamental seems rather soft, but with a less intense fundamental and more intense harmonics, the sound rather appears hollow. You can also notice that some voices seem nasal and other sounds seem strident. Also, two notes played together seem dissonant and melodious, depending on distance (in Hz) between them.

In closing, it should be recalled that the pleasure afforded by the sounds of music can also depend on cultural habits and factors associated with learning. Complex music (e.g., symphonies or operas) are more difficult to enjoy, but with repeated exposure to a certain piece (some learning), it becomes more accessible (see Chapter 3).

2.4   Biological Bases

Between the arrival of a sound wave to the ear and the capture by the brain of an intelligible and revealing message, a long path is traveled. The waves of compressions and rarefactions included within the initial stimulus are translated through various stages that constitute the path from the external ear to the inner ear, via the middle ear.

2.4.1   Outer, Middle, and Inner Ear

The outer ear includes essentially two parts, the pinna and the auditory canal (Fig. 2.4). The function of the pinna is to collect sound waves and to direct them into the auditory canal. However, the role of the pinna, if we consider its lack of mobility, is much less important in humans than in some other vertebrates. Nevertheless, it serves to amplify sounds, especially those falling within a range of 1.5–7 kHz and, to a certain extent, contributes to locating the direction of sounds (Chap. 3).

The ear canal is a passageway that extends for about 2.5–3 cm from pinna to the eardrum. Throughout this duct, which has a diameter of about 0.75 cm, there are glands that secrete a wax, technically known as cerumen, which serves as a barrier for protecting the inner ear from dust and dirt.

Between the outer ear and the middle ear, there is a thin membrane, the eardrum, covering a surface of approximately 70 mm^2. The function of the middle ear is to ensure the transmission of the air movement from the eardrum to the inner ear. This transmission takes place via three tiny bones, called the ossicles: the malleus (hammer), the incus (anvil), and the stapes (stirrup). The malleus is attached to the eardrum; the incus is connected to the malleus and the stapes, and the stapes is attached to a small structure, the oval window (or vestibular window), which is the gateway through which the air vibrations are transmitted to the inner ear. The base of the stapes has a surface area of only 3 mm^2.

The inner ear contains an important amount of liquid. For transmitting the wave from an air medium to a liquid medium, it is necessary to overcome a certain amount

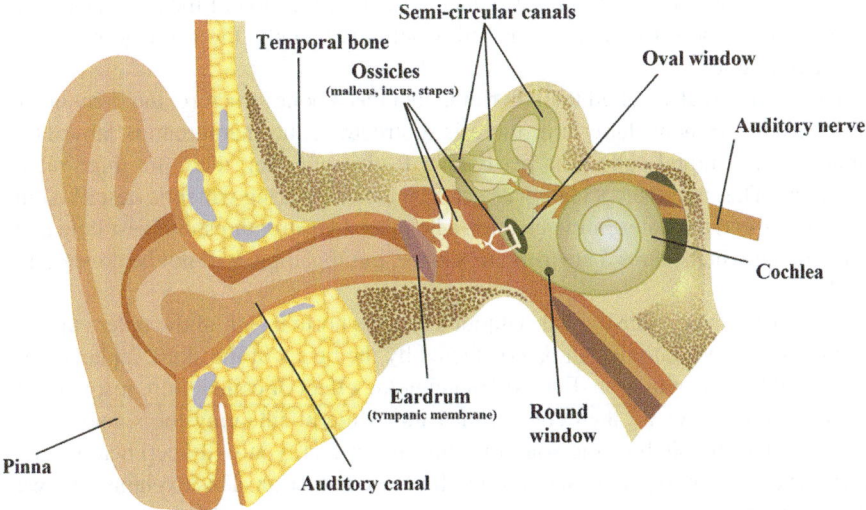

Fig. 2.4 General sketch of the outer ear, middle ear, and inner ear; illustrated here with the semicircular canals, which are parts of the inner ear, but serve a function other than hearing, namely, the sense of balance (Figure by Leila Aazari)

of resistance. The fact of transmitting the vibrations from a large area, that of the eardrum, to a small area, that is the one at the base of the stapes, results in a significant increase of the pressure and allows to transmit effectively the information provided by the air vibrations. The main role of the middle ear is therefore to contribute to the production of this pressure when the vibrations are entering into the inner ear through the oval window.

Just below the oval window is the round window (or cochlear window). This is part of the inner ear, but its function is closely linked to the activity of the oval window. With the fluid in the ear being incompressible, any pressure on the oval window has to be absorbed elsewhere, which is made possible by the round window which is actually an elastic membrane.

Other structures that are parts of the middle ear contribute directly to the functioning of hearing. A structure called the Eustachian tube (or internal auditory meatus) connects the middle ear to the pharynx and to the nose or mouth. Its role is to make the air pressure in the middle ear equal to that existing in the ear canal. It is possible to notice the need to equilibrate that pressure when climbing in altitude or traveling in an airplane, which is made possible by swallowing or yawning. The air may then be sent from the pharynx to the middle ear, which enables the eardrum to vibrate normally.

Two muscles also have a key role in modulating the transmission of sound energy to the inner ear. One is called the tensor tympani muscle and the other is the stapedius muscle. They allow the release of the stapes from the oval window. The function of these two muscles is to protect the auditory system when sounds are too intense. Thus, while the middle ear is built so as to overcome the resistance of the liquid medium of the inner ear by increasing the pressure, it also has a security system, when sounds are too loud, for reducing the transmission of these sounds. The contraction of these two muscles is reflex activity, namely, the acoustic reflex or attenuation reflex.

The inner ear, also called the labyrinth, contains a bone structure, the bony labyrinth. Inside the bony labyrinth, there is a structure, the membranous labyrinth, immersed in a liquid called the perilymph. In the inner ear, there are three main structures. The first, the cochlea, has a crucial role in hearing which is described in the next section and later in the chapter. The other two structures, the vestibule and semicircular canals, have a key role in balance, but this topic will not be covered in this book.

Note that it is possible to hear without using the normal path of the outer ear and the middle ear. Vibrations can be conducted by the bones of the skull, a phenomenon called bone conduction. For experiencing the effect of conduction, just make a sound continuously and then cover your ears (while maintaining the sound). You will hear that the pitch of the sound is shifting. In fact, you will keep hearing the sound, even with plugged ears, but through bone conduction. This explains why we often feel we do not recognize our own voice on a recording. When we speak, we are hearing both the sounds that are transmitted via the outer ear and the middle ear and sound transmitted by bone conduction. The sound transmitted through bone conduction is not present when you hear a recording of your voice.

2.4.2   The Cochlea

The cochlea has the shape of a spiral, a kind of snail which is completing about two and a half turns. It contains a long membranous tube, the cochlear duct in which flows a liquid called endolymph.

Essentially, the cochlea is divided into three parts by two membranes (Fig. 2.5). Above the cochlear duct is the vestibular canal separated from the cochlear duct by a thin membrane called Reissner's membrane (or vestibular membrane). Below the basilar membrane, there is the tympanic canal in which flows, as is the case for the vestibular canal, the perilymph. Both canals communicate with each other through a narrow channel, the helicotrema.

When there are sound vibrations, they are transmitted to the perilymph. The fluid movement thus transmitted travels along the vestibular canal and returns to the tympanic canal. This movement then generates an oscillation of the basilar membrane which thus undergoes different deformations. The basilar membrane is narrower and stiffer at the base, close to the oval window and where the sound signals reach the cochlea, than on its apex.

It is actually on this basilar membrane that we find the spiral organ, also called the organ of Corti. In particular, it contains receptor cells that convert sound waves into action potentials. The organ of Corti is composed of thousands of hair cells. These cells, lying on supporting cells called Deiters' cells, each contain dozens of stereocilia. There are two types of hair cells, inner and outer. There are about 3500 inner hair cells in each ear, arranged on the same row, and more than 10,000 outer hair cells, arranged in three rows. Yet more than 90 % of the 30,000 afferent fibers of the auditory nerve are connected with inner hair cells, whereas approximately 500 efferent fibers (from the brain) of the auditory nerve are connected to the outer hair cells. When the basilar membrane oscillates, it is the contact of the stereocilia with the tectorial membrane, which is located just above the sensory cells, that is the

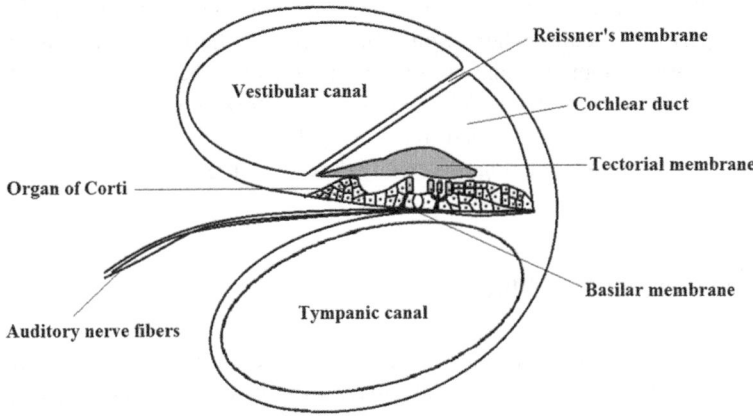

Fig. 2.5 Cross section of the cochlea

basis of hearing. It is at this point that all the mechanical vibration (first in air and then in the liquid medium of the inner ear) is converted into an electrical signal, nerve impulse, that the brain can recognize.

2.4.3 Central Mechanisms

Because they involve many crossings and relays, pathways bringing information from the cochlea to the auditory cortex are relatively complex. Auditory information enters into the brain at the bulb level (see Appendix C). The nerve impulses travel from the spiral ganglia to the brain structures by the vestibulocochlear nerves (the eighth cranial nerve) which split into two branches. In a given ear, the information is routed to the ventral and dorsal parts of the cochlear nucleus. From the cochlear nucleus, different routes can be followed. The neurons of the ventral part will make connection with the superior olivary nucleus, one-half traveling in the opposite half of the brain (contralateral side) and the other half remaining in the ipsilateral side. Early in the auditory system, at the olivary level (at the level of the medulla oblongata), there is a representation of the activity of both ears on each side of the brain.

The axons of the neurons in the dorsal cochlear nucleus all reach the *inferior colliculus* (at the level of the midbrain) on the contralateral side. Information from the superior olivary structure reaching the inferior colliculus originates from both the left ventral cochlear nucleus and the right ventral cochlear nucleus. Note that some fibers from the contralateral superior olivary structure and some fibers from the dorsal cochlear nucleus will transit through the nucleus of the medial lemniscus before reaching the inferior colliculus; moreover, at the level of this latter structure, many nerve fibers are crossing.

The nerve impulse is then routed to the thalamus, more specifically at the *median geniculate nucleus*, for eventually arriving at the *primary auditory cortex*, or A1, in the temporal lobe. Note that there are some relays between the inferior colliculus and the superior colliculus where would be processed the information about the location of a sound source, along with information from other sensory modalities. Finally, it should be noted that in A1, there is a *tonotopic organization*, i.e., a spatial representation of the different sound frequencies. In fact, this organization exists at all stages of auditory information processing described above.

2.5 Theories of Hearing

The previous section allowed to learn the role of different biological structures in the path of the sound wave from the pinna to the auditory cortex. However, the question remains as to how these waves can afford to hear with so many nuances. Researchers have long addressed this yet simple question: how can we perceive pitch? What is happening exactly on the basilar membrane, in the organ of Corti? The next subsections provide an overview of the main answers revealed by research in the field of hearing.

2.5.1 Frequency Theory

The initial theoretical explanation based on the idea of the frequency was proposed by the English physiologist William Rutherford. In the past, telephones were built with a diaphragm, and it was the vibrations of this device, caused by the voice, that were converted into electrical signals. Once reaching the acoustic of another telephone, the signals were reproduced. Rutherford tried to draw a parallel between the basilar membrane and the diaphragm. According to him, the basilar membrane would serve to reproduce the pressure variations transmitted by the stapes. From such a perspective, the auditory nerve serves as a transmission cable, and the role of the brain is to interpret the frequency.

This formulation of the frequency theory was not going to hold the road. The basilar membrane is not like the diaphragm of a telephone was. The basilar membrane is not of the same width throughout and rigidity changes from one place to another. An even more serious objection to the original frequency theory is the simple fact that the ear is sensitive to frequencies ranging up to 20 kHz. This implies that a nerve fiber would have to be able to send 20,000 impulses per second. In fact, even the transmission of sound of 1000 Hz is problematic because a nerve cell cannot produce 1000 impulses per second. In short, this theory cannot account for the perception of all pitches associated with the audible frequency range. In other words, understanding the perception of high frequencies causes problem.

One solution to this problem was proposed by Wever and Bray (1937). This solution, which is based on the idea of cooperation between the nerve fibers, is called the *volley principle*. According to this principle, the neural activity associated with each of the different cycles of a sound is distributed via a series of fibers. Each fiber does not have to respond to every cycle of a sound wave. After a response to a cycle, a fiber has a recovery period and another fiber responds to the next cycle (Fig. 2.6). Indeed, a large number of fibers share the work. It is the grouped activity on a set of fibers that captures all cycles of a given sound wave. Finally, the volley principle accounts not only for the perception of pitch but also for that of loudness. The perception of loudness is accounted by the combined activity of more than one fiber for each cycle of the sound wave.

In fact, we now know that the activity of an auditory nerve fiber is generated when, in a given cycle, the wave is at its highest pressure level. So there is synchronization between the pressure change caused by a stimulus and the beginning of nerve activity. This phenomenon is called *phase locking*. Moreover, a neuron does not have to trigger its activity in each cycle, but when it does, it always happens at the same point in the cycle. This phenomenon also means that there is in the auditory nerve fiber a temporal code related to a sound wave. Due to the refractory period required for each fiber of the auditory nerve, the temporal coding begins to be a little less reliable for frequencies above 1000 Hz and becomes virtually useless with frequencies above 5000 Hz.

2.5.2 Theories Based on Location

The idea of associating the processing of auditory information with a particular place on the basilar membrane is not new. Already in the nineteenth century, the German physiologist Hermann von Helmholtz proposed a theory of "the place of resonance" to explain the perception of pitch. Knowing that the width of the basilar membrane is not the same everywhere, he believed that, at a given location, the membrane, due to its width, would give a sound of a particular pitch, just like the strings of a piano, being of different lengths, give different notes. The analogy with the piano was proved to be incorrect, but the idea of linking the pitch to a specific place on the basilar membrane remains relevant. It is the basis of the place theory: there is indeed a tonotopic organization of hair cells in the organ of Corti. In other words, there is a spatial coding of frequency. Some frequencies are processed at specific locations on the basilar membrane.

Nobel Prize laureate in Physiology and Medicine in 1961, physicist Georg von Békésy described the mechanics inside the cochlea that underlies this spatial encoding. As we have seen earlier, the basilar membrane is narrow and rigid at the base of the cochlea, and, closer to its apex, it gradually widens and becomes less rigid (Fig. 2.6). Thus, when the stapes transmits the vibrations within the inner ear, this causes a hydrodynamic movement. The sound wave is thus propagated from one end of the basilar membrane to the other. This wave motion along the membrane constitutes the traveling wave.

The maximum point of displacement of the wave depends on its frequency. Indeed, this maximum point, that is the point where the basilar membrane is the more curved (Fig. 2.7), is nearest to the helicotrema if the frequency is low. The

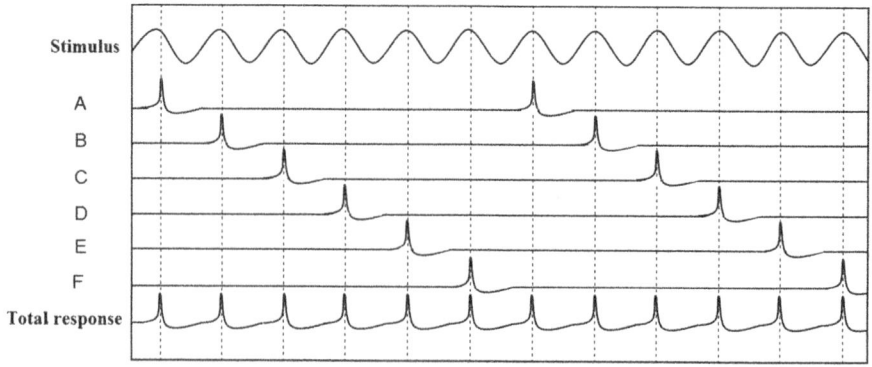

Fig. 2.6 Illustration of the volley principle, with all fibers (**A–F**) combined on the *bottom curve*

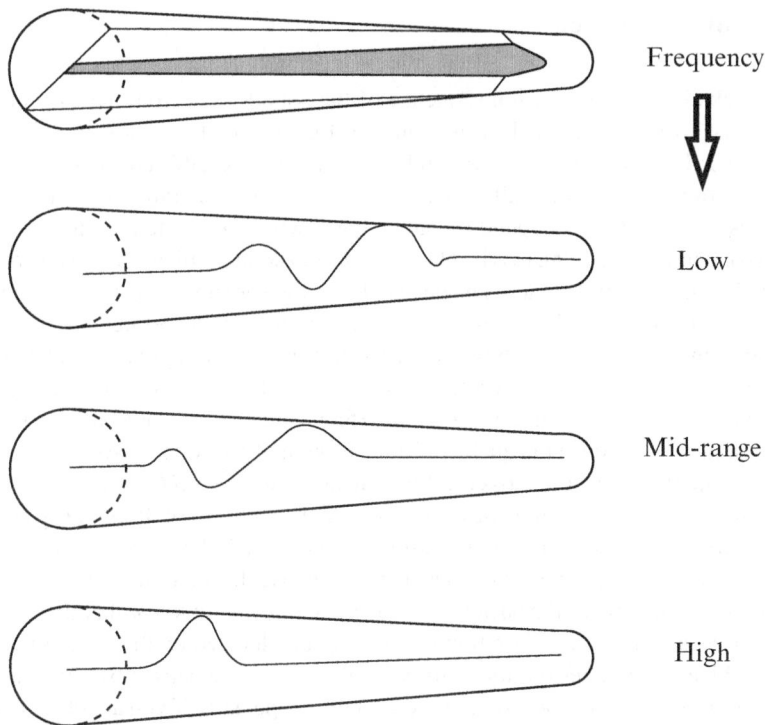

Frequency

Low

Mid-range

High

Fig. 2.7 On *top*, a representation of the basilar membrane (in *gray*) when the cochlea is unrolled; *bottom figures* illustrate the different points of maximum displacement of the traveling wave as a function of the sound frequencies

wave rapidly reaches its maximum amplitude and then quickly disappears. Conversely, the maximum point of displacement is reached farther away on the basilar membrane if the frequency is high. It is where the membrane is the most curved that the hair cells are the most displaced and generate the highest stimulation. The waves of different frequencies therefore will have their maximum impact on different parts of the basilar membrane, and the auditory nerve fibers stimulated will transmit their specific information to the auditory cortex.

This explanation of von Békésy based on the idea of a traveling wave allows not only to understand the perception of pitch but also the perception of loudness. Loudness would indeed depend on the magnitude of the traveling wave. Greater sound intensity provokes larger movement amplitudes on the basilar membrane. Larger amplitude affects more hair cells and produces greater inclination of these cells; therefore, larger amplitude results in more neural activity.

Note in closing this section that the frequency theory (volley principle) and the place theory (traveling wave) are both accepted. It is generally recognized that for low frequencies, the volley principle applies (frequency coding), and for high frequencies, the traveling wave hypothesis applies (spatial coding).

2.6   Clinical Aspects

Some breaks in the transmission sequence of the sound wave from the eardrum to the auditory cortex can cause hearing damage. Besides the fact that some diseases can be caused by damage to central auditory pathways or different regions of the auditory cortex—sometimes called *central deafness*—we generally distinguish two categories of hearing loss, depending on the place where the deficit is caused.

A first category of hearing loss is related to *transmission* problems (or *conduction*). Essentially, this type of disorder is mechanical, i.e., the sound wave is not transmitted efficiently to the cochlea. The causes of such a condition are therefore located at the outer ear or in the middle ear. These causes range from an excessive accumulation of wax to the deterioration of the ossicles. Similarly, throat infections, connected by the Eustachian tube to the middle ear, may interfere with the pressure balance in the middle ear and thus reduce the quality of transmission of the sound wave.

The second type of hearing loss is referred to as *sensorineural* (or *perceptive deafness*). This problem is caused by deterioration of the cochlea or of the auditory nerve. This deterioration occurs for various reasons such as metabolic problems or trauma. Some medications with toxic properties may also cause this kind of disorder.

Still about sensorineural hearing loss, it is most relevant to know that this deficit may occur as a result of deterioration of the hair cells located on the organ of Corti in the cochlea. Such deterioration is irreversible and can be caused by exposure to sounds of high intensity. The stronger the sounds—especially if you are close to the sound source—the less exposure time it takes to incur permanent damage. Therefore, there is a high price to pay when we offer ourselves this wonderful luxury of listening to loud music, often directly from the source using headphones!

If you are exposed, for instance, to sounds of approximately 85 dB, about 8 h per day, at some point you will affect your hearing. Exposure to loudness causes hearing fatigue, i.e., a shift of the detection threshold for a given period. The effects are the same, for example, (1) with an exposure to 88-dB sounds for 4 h per day or (2) with an exposure to 100-dB noise for 15 min per day. However, repeated exposure to even louder sounds may cause permanent threshold shift. Note that a loud sound might sound weaker after a few minutes of exposure. This phenomenon is called auditory adaptation.

The hearing abilities change with age. Indeed, age causes a loss of hearing called *presbycusis*. In particular, as we get older, the detection threshold for high frequencies becomes much higher. Consequently, it is possible for young persons to receive an audible signal indicating the arrival of a text message on their phone without an adult of a certain age (e.g., a teacher!) hearing it. It is unlikely that an adult over 40 years will hear a sound above 15 kHz or an adult over 50 years will hear a sound above 12 kHz. High frequencies have even been used to get rid of noisy teenagers loitering in a schoolyard.

Finally, among the quite severe disorders connected somehow to hearing, there is *tinnitus*. This problem consists of an impression that a sound or noise is present, even in the absence of any external auditory stimulation. Tinnitus can sound like whistling or rustling and can be caused by several factors. The sound may be continuous or intermittent and is usually rather acute. Tinnitus can indicate the presence of a hearing disorder caused by damage to the cochlea, for example, or occur after noise trauma or during an infection.

Chapter 3
Hearing

Understanding how we hear cannot be reduced to a mere description of facts based on physics and on a description of the structures of the ear or brain involved in hearing. What we hear is full of shades and impressions. These shades come in particular from the way of organizing the auditory information that reaches the ear, this organization being based on certain principles. We also use cues to find out where sounds are coming from. Just as if all this was not mysterious enough, some sounds appear clearly identifiable as speech sounds, while other sounds clearly appear as part of a musical structure. The purpose of this chapter is to understand these sets of auditory phenomena.

3.1 Perceptual Organization

As we will see in the study of vision, major principles revealing how visual perception is organized have been uncovered almost a century ago. The development on the perceptual organization in audition came a little later. Albert Bregman has contributed greatly to the development of this facet of the hearing, particularly with the publication of his book *Auditory Scene Analysis*, which provides a solid synthesis of the principles underlying this organization (Bregman, 1990).

A series of illusions or auditory effects show that the link between what is presented and what is heard is not always straightforward. The brain has to deal with the entire context in which the stimuli are arriving. In particular, the extent to which stimuli are similar and arrive more or less at the same time determines what is heard.

© Springer International Publishing Switzerland 2016
S. Grondin, *Psychology of Perception*, DOI 10.1007/978-3-319-31791-5_3

3.1.1   Streaming

The organization of auditory information is the perceptual integration and segregation of the auditory material of the environment in significant auditory representations (Snyder & Alain, 2007). When there are many sounds in the environment that arrive simultaneously or in rapid succession, it is necessary that elements be grouped, integrated, and merged into the same "sound object," just like other components of the auditory environment that have to be segregated and assigned to different "objects." Indeed, while the sound may sometimes refer to the physical stimulation in the environment or to the experience extracted from it by an observer, Bregman will use the term *stream* to describe the perceptual unit forming an object. The stream, or auditory line, is the psychological experience in audition that could be compared to the notion of object in vision.

The auditory stream allows the grouping of related acoustical qualities; it is based on the relationships that one perceives between successive sounds. The concept of grouping is central to the idea covered by this notion of stream. A musical melody and the sounds of successive and regular footsteps are striking examples of impressions of streams. In the environment, there are many changes of sound intensities and frequencies and changes of source locations and several temporal irregularities. However, the proximity of the frequencies of different sounds and their patterns over time are very strong factors leading to the formation of streams because they give the impression that the sounds go together.

So, if two sounds of different frequencies are presented in succession repeatedly, they are spontaneously grouped and perceived as parts of the same structure, or of the same stream, if these frequencies are not too far apart from each other (Fig. 3.1, upper panels). However, if these frequencies are too distant from each other (Fig. 3.1, lower panels), the sounds are segregated as if they would belong to distinct streams (Miller, 1947).

Along the same line, it is possible to generate an impression of rhythm, like galloping, for instance, when the first and third sounds of a sequence of three have the same frequency, while the second one has a different frequency (Fig. 3.2). This effect occurs when the three sounds are close in time (van Noorden, 1975). If this sequence is heard twice, but the frequency of the first and third sounds becomes quite different from that of the second sound, the galloping impression disappears and two distinct streams are heard.

3.1.2   Illusion of Continuity and Gap Transfer

The illusion of continuity is also an important element contributing to the auditory scene. This illusion consists of a sound interrupted by a silent gap, but a sound for which we perceive continuity when the gap is filled with more intense noise (Fig. 3.3). Thus, the presence of a loud noise instead of a silent gap gives the impression

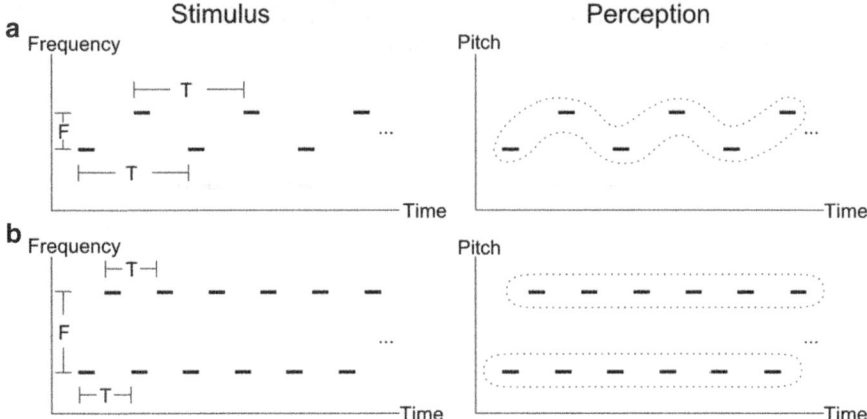

Fig. 3.1 Segregation of auditory stream as a function of the proximity of the frequencies and of the proximity in time. Two sounds of different frequencies, which are alternately repeated, are perceived as if they were two streams (**b**), rather than only one (**a**), when the frequencies are quite distant from each other (*F* is large). Segregation is facilitated when the sounds of the same frequency are much closer to each other in time (*T* is small)

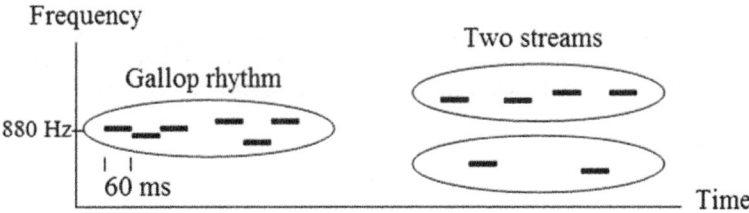

Fig. 3.2 *Left*: impression of gallop caused by proximity in time and frequency. *Right*: if the frequency of the first and third sounds is too far from the frequency of the second, the gallop impression is replaced by the impression that there are two separate streams

that the sound, though interrupted, is continuous. This illusion is essentially a sound restoration, and such restoration effects also occur for speech and music (Sasaki, 1980; Warren, 1970). For instance, the missing parts in a sentence could prevent someone from understanding its meaning, but replacing these parts by noises would allow recovering the meaning.

Another phenomenon showing how an auditory scene is organized is called the *gap transfer* illusion. It differs from the previous illusion, although it also implies an impression of continuity. This time, the illusion occurs when sounds are continuously changing in frequency. As illustrated in Fig. 3.4, the illusion can be generated with two sounds of different durations, having a frequency progression in opposite directions and intersecting at their center. If the longer segment is interrupted, the interruption is perceived as belonging to the shorter one. In other words, even if, physically, the short sound is continuous, it is this sound that will be perceived as

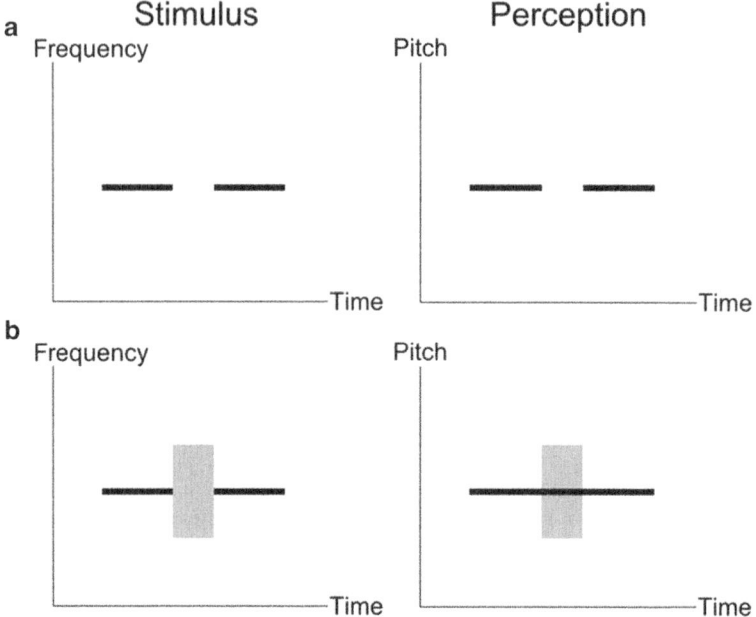

Fig. 3.3 The illusion of auditory continuity. A sound with a silent interruption (**a**) is perceived as being continuous when the interruption is filled with another sound (**b**). The occurrence of this illusion is possible only when the sound inserted is more intense than the discontinuous sound

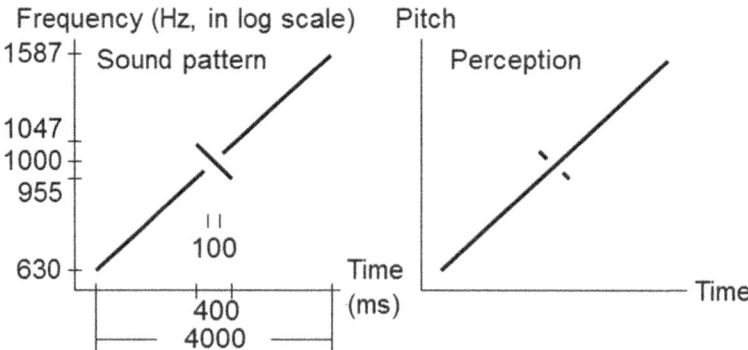

Fig. 3.4 Illustration of the gap transfer illusion. At the perceptual level, the interruption is assigned to the short rather than to the long segment, as is the case physically (see Nakajima et al., 2000)

interrupted (Nakajima et al., 2000).[1] Indeed, although it is the longer sound that is interrupted, it keeps being perceived as continuous. In brief, the long and short sounds are physically continuous and discontinuous, respectively, but are rather perceptually perceived as discontinuous and continuous, respectively.

It is interesting to note the following special case of gap transfer illusion. It can be generated with a synthetic sound, the letter /a/, where a long /a/ and a short /a/ intersect, and where, as was the case earlier, the long sound is interrupted. Once again, it is the long sound that appears to be continuous and the short one that seems discontinuous. However, this illusion does not occur if different vowels intersect (Kuroda, Nakajima, Tsunashima, & Yasutake, 2009). If the vowel /i/ is short and intersects with a long /a/, it is the latter that will be perceived as interrupted and the /i/ will be perceived as continuous. In other words, there is an agreement between the physical properties of the stimuli and what is perceived. Consequently, no gap transfer illusion occurs. Indeed, the illusion with synthetic vowels occurs only when both sounds are identical vowels or have the same spectral structure.

There are, of course, many other auditory special effects. One of the most classic ones is the Shepard staircase which consists of a series of looping tones appearing to increase in frequency continuously. The same effect can be obtained in the opposite direction: an impression that the frequency of the sound appears to decrease without interruption, even if it is a sound loop that is used (see Deutsch, 2010[2]). Indeed, this illusion could be compared to that proposed by Penrose for vision, but in the auditory modality (Fig. 3.5, Penrose & Penrose, 1958). In this visual illusion, it is possible to imagine someone going upstairs forever or downstairs forever.

3.2 Sound Location

For some species, hearing is to some extent a way to see, and this is due to the efficiency for localizing what is present in the environment. This capability is called echolocation and can occur in the air, as for bats, or in water, as for dolphins.

In humans, the ability to localize sounds in space is perhaps not as critical or vital as it is for other animals. However, this ability contributes to the production of fine representations of what surrounds us in the auditory environment. It is possible, by using several cues, to obtain quite accurate information concerning which direction sounds are coming from and, to some extent, how far away the source of these sounds is.

---

[1] It is possible to get interesting demonstrations of different acoustical effects, for instance:

Bregman, A. S., & Ahad, P. A. (1996). *Demonstrations of auditory scene analysis: The perceptual organization of sound* [CD]. Cambridge, MA: MIT Press.

Moreover, it is possible to access these demonstrations on different web sites. We recommend:

Nakajima, Y. (2000). *Demonstrations of auditory illusions and tricks* (2nd ed.) [http://www.design.kyushuu.ac.jp/~ynhome/ENG/Demo/illusions2nd.html].

[2] The reader is invited to discover several acoustical illusions or auditory paradoxes on Diana Deutsch's web site: [http://deutsch.ucsd.edu/psychology/pages.php?i=201#Introduction.php].

Fig. 3.5 Visual illustration
of Shepard's auditory
illusion with a classic
visual illusion, the
impossible Penrose stairs

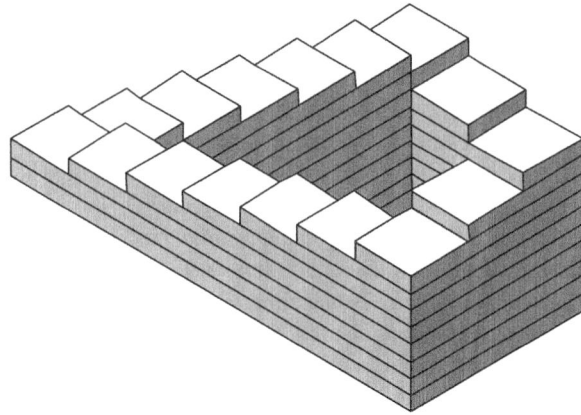

3.2.1   *Location of Direction*

If you close your eyes and listen to what is around you, localizing sounds may seem
so obvious to you that you may even wonder if there is any need to study the question. If you hear footsteps, the sound of shoes or heels on a hard surface, you will
rapidly be informed, without looking, that a person approaches or moves away from
you. As well, if someone wishes to capture your attention by calling you by your
name, you will very likely turn your head in the right direction. You will know if the
sound comes from the left or from the right, on a horizontal plane, and you will also
know if it comes from above or below. You will turn automatically in the direction of
the sound source, probably to direct your gaze toward it. This capacity is due in part
to the pinna as it contributes, for instance, to the localization of high-frequency
sounds (Musicant & Butler, 1984) and to providing cues that the brain can interpret.

A powerful cue for knowing the direction a sound is coming from is related to
the arrival time to each ear. This cue, called *interaural time difference*, is based on
the fact that sounds from one source often arrive at a different time to each ear.
Sounds emitted from your right arrive at your right ear before reaching the left
ear. This difference may seem minimal, given the small distance between the ears
(the size of one's head). Nevertheless, the brain finds a way to use this difference
and to extract some meaning of it. If the sound reaches your left ear first, the brain
will conclude that the sound source is closer to your left ear than to your right ear.
This cue is particularly effective for locating low-frequency sounds (Wightman &
Kistler, 1992).

That said, in addition to the arrival time in each ear, per se, the brain also takes
into account, for locating sounds, the point of the cycle at which a sound reaches
each ear. This cue, called the *phase difference* to each ear, would also contribute to
the localization of low-frequency sounds.

Another important cue for localizing sounds is provided by the fact that they do
not necessarily arrive at each ear with the same intensity. This phenomenon can be
easily demonstrated. Ask someone speaking loudly to you, directly into your left or

into your right ear. You will soon discover the need to mute the sound on one side more than on the other side! Along the same line, if you are walking on a sidewalk and a noisy motorcycle or a fire truck with a high-pitch siren is near you, or if a worker is using a jackhammer nearby, you will quickly understand that one ear, the one closest to the noise source, needs more protection than the other.

Indeed, the intensity difference at each ear when a sound arrives directly from one side is due to the fact that the head causes what is called a partial sound shadow. This shadow, which allows an attenuation of sound intensity, is most effective for higher frequencies. Moreover, because humans do not have a mobile pinna as some other species do, it remains possible to rotate the head in one direction or another for localizing sounds more efficiently. Such movements produce slight variations in relative intensities or arrival times to each ear, improving the capability to determine where the sound comes from.

If experimental conditions are set so that the interaural time difference and the interaural intensity difference or the pinna provide contradictory information, the information based on the interaural time difference will prevail if the sound includes low-frequency components. Without low frequencies, the apparent direction of sounds will be based on the intensity differences or the pinna (Wightman & Kistler, 1992). The term *head transfer function* is used to describe the cues based on binaural perception, the differences in intensity in each ear being much greater than the time difference when the sound source is nearby, i.e., less than one meter away (Brungart, Durlach, & Rabinowitz, 1999).

3.2.2   Location of Distance

It is possible to get quite an accurate idea of the direction a sound is coming from; however, estimating accurately the distance from a sound source is quite difficult. Determining roughly whether the source is near or far is relatively easy, but quantifying the actual distance is a much more difficult exercise, and we rarely try. We do try to determine, for example, whether the thunderclap we have just heard is more or less distant. Indeed, the intensity of a sound reveals right away if it is more or less distant, a loud sound being most often very close. If you know the intensity at the sound source, it becomes possible to get a good approximation of the distance based on the perceived intensity.

Indeed, the function linking the loudness and the distance, D, between the source and an observer is the following one: $1/D^2$. Because sound pressure is a function of the square root of intensity, the pressure decreases with the distance according to the equation $1/D$. Consequently, this results in the following simple rule: sound pressure decreases by about 6 dB every time the distance between an observer and a sound source is doubled. This relationship, $1/D$, holds however only under special circumstances. First, it does not apply when an observer is very close to the source (Butler, Levy, & Neff, 1980). Moreover, it applies only where the sound is emitted from a specific place and in free-field environments, i.e., free of obstructions. These conditions are indeed rarely the ones encountered in daily life.

Another very important cue can be used for revealing the distance separating an observer from a sound source. This cue is the ratio of the amount of sound arriving at the ear directly from a sound source and the amount of sound arriving at the ear after hitting an obstacle. Reverberations are sounds that have bounced after hitting a surface, before reaching the ear. When the environment is filled with more reverberations, it leads to an impression of echo. This is a distinctive quality that can be perceived. As the distance between an observer and a sound source increases, the presence of obstacles along the way becomes more likely. Thus, the ratio between the sounds coming directly from the source and those from reverberations decreases as the distance between the source and the observer increases (Larsen, Iyer, Lansing, & Feng, 2008).

Indeed, sounds consisting mainly of high frequencies seem to arrive from a near-distance source, whereas those consisting mainly of low frequencies seem to come from farther away. This could be easily understood considering that high frequencies are more easily blocked when obstacles are on the way between the source and the ear. Considering how distance affects the quality of sound, and considering the important differences of sound intensities with distance, one can easily imagine how difficult it is to build concert halls or sport centers that would preserve a high quality of sounds for everyone seating in such buildings.

Everyday life is also filled with several acoustic phenomena that one might well encounter at some moment. Frequency changes occurring with moving cars or trucks with a siren (police or ambulance) generate a special auditory impression called the Doppler effect. Indeed, sounds are rarely static. Sound sources are often moving, and sometimes, it is the observer that is moving. As a car approaches, frequencies sound higher than they really are; nearby, there are no inconsistencies between what is emitted and what is perceived, but as the car moves away, perceived frequencies seem lower than they really are.

Considering that the perception of distance in everyday life depends heavily on vision, it is not surprising to see the large influence exerted by this sensory mode on the impression of distance or direction of sound sources. You likely know the phenomenon called *ventriloquism*, which refers, for instance, to the impression that a voice comes from the mouth of a puppet moving lips, even though you know that the voice does not come from that mouth: it comes from a source nearby, the puppeteer. Along the same line, even though the voices in cinema or on television do not come from the mouth of the characters' moving lips, but from speakers located nearby, you rarely experience the impression that the sound does not come from the person talking, except if the movements of the lips and the arrival of the sounds are not well synchronized.

Note finally that we sometimes get the impression that thunder and lightning, which are indeed occurring together, at the same moment, are not synchronized. That could be explained by the fact that the sound travels more slowly than light. If lightning is far away, the gap between thunder and lightning is great. Indeed, if you ever feel that this gap is getting smaller after a few minutes, you can conclude that lightning is getting closer to you.

3.3   Hearing Music

Sometimes, a series of consecutive sounds simply produce noise. But on some occasions, a series of sounds produce what is called music. Whether or not it is music, these sounds could be described on the basis of their pitch, loudness, and timbre. But why do certain sounds result in an impression of music? They need to be linked according to some specific structure.

3.3.1   Technical Description

While sounds usually vary according to their pitch, musical pitch is particular as it falls on a chromatic scale. The musical pitch has a certain height (for instance, a more or less high pitch) and is located somewhere (the note) on an octave. The octave is an interval separating eight notes and is composed of 12 semitones. For a given note, the ratio from one octave to another in terms of frequencies is simple: it doubles or is divided by two. In brief, sounds that are one octave apart have the same name.

Indeed, the magic of music is that two sounds separated by one octave seem similar. For instance, if one plays eight consecutive notes on a keyboard (do, re, mi, fa, sol, la, ti, do or C, D, E, F, G, A, B, C), one octave is covered (note that D to D, E to E, etc. also covers one octave). Even if the frequency of one C is much higher than that of another C, we can recognize the similarity between these two notes. However, although F and G are on the same octave and are very close to each other, we do not recognize them as quite similar. But if two different Gs are played together, they are not dissonant. When describing musical sounds, it not sufficient to only talk about the fact that they are more or less high pitches. There is a need to take into account the fact that they do have some similarity, a feature referred to as *chroma*.

Figure 3.6 illustrates the range of frequencies covered by the piano. This figure identifies the notes, their frequency, and the ranges of frequencies covered by certain musical instruments and human voices. A human voice can hardly cover more than two octaves, but humans can nevertheless hear, as indicated in Chap. 2, sounds ranging roughly from 20 Hz to 20 kHz, i.e., ten octaves.

A chord is the superposition of more than two sounds according to certain rules. It is only in the middle of the sixteenth century that the notion of interval was replaced by the notion of chord (Honegger, 1976). Nowadays, the impression of music and the psychological impression left by a chord do not correspond at all to the impression that would give only two of the notes of a chord. In other words, if a chord consists in notes C, E, and G, it cannot be reduced to the succession of C with G, C with E, and E with G.

We should count for instance dynamics and rhythm among the other important concepts that contribute to shape the impression of music. The former is the difference

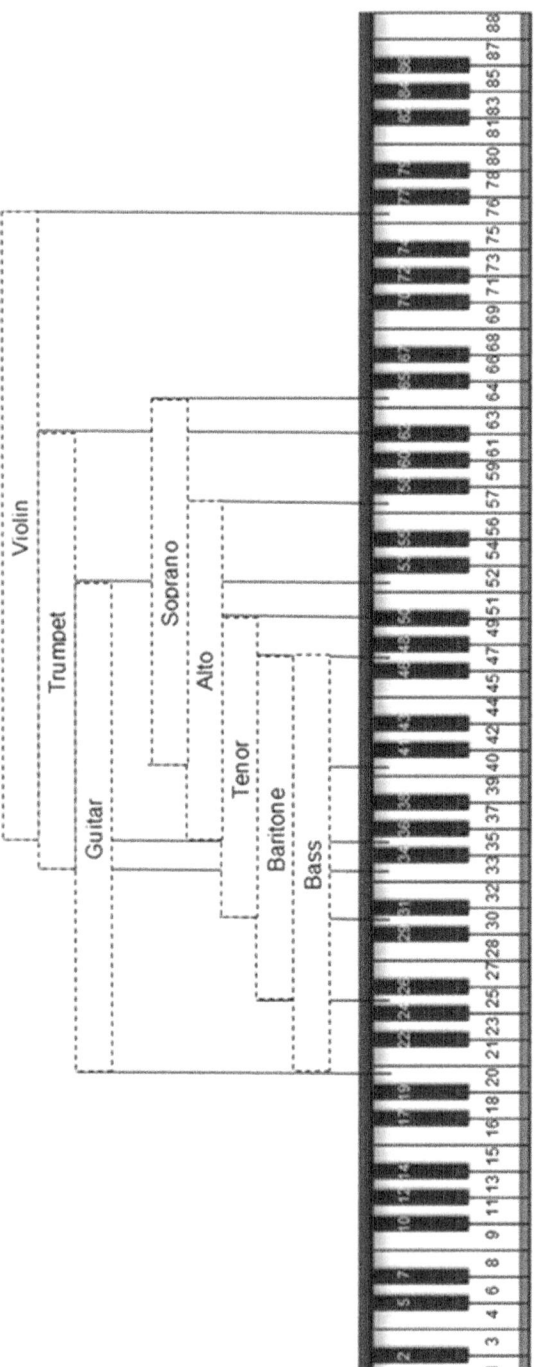

Fig. 3.6 Range of frequencies covered by the piano and comparison with human voices and other musical instruments. For each number (1–88) under the keyboard, there is a number indicating the frequency of the note (in Hz)

between the levels of loudness. Musicians sometimes refer to shade or musical contrast when describing dynamics. Rhythm designates the perceptual organization over time; it is closely linked to the duration of relatively short or long successive notes. Several expressions are used in order to designate the duration of a note (e.g., quaver, quarter, half, whole). Given the ubiquity of time in music, it is not surprising that musicians are better than nonmusicians for detecting slight temporal differences in musical excerpts (Grondin & Laforest, 2004) or for keeping track of time by counting or singing (Grondin & Killeen, 2009). Note that rhythm and tempo should not be confused. The latter term refers to the speed used for performing a musical piece. For instance, tempo could be *allegro* or *adagio*, the Italian terms for fast and slow tempi, respectively.

A series of very brief elements can form a leitmotiv, which provides a characteristic to what is called a musical phrase. On a more global scale, a melody is formed by the successive pitch variations of the different notes. Consequently, a melody is not perceived as a series of successive individual and distinct sounds, but rather as coherent entity or whole. This idea of whole is not without reminding the principles of sound organization, described earlier, and the organization of form that will be described in Chap. 6 on the visual perception of form.

3.3.2 Subjective Experience

Liking or disliking a given combination of sounds that can be easily recognized as being music does not depend just on the fact of using some particular physical features. Many factors contribute to the subjective appreciation of music. The specific musical tradition and habits are some of these factors. At an individual level, habits are particularly critical, which does not prevent from remaining open to new musical styles. Indeed, habit generates familiarity, which sometimes turns out to be determinant. Just consider how many times you may not have liked a musical piece the first time you listened to it, but finally liked it after a few repetitions. It is much easier to appreciate a given voice or musical style when you can recognize it. What might sound like great music for those used to a given style may well sound dissonant for those less familiar with this style.

Restricting music appreciation to familiarity would leave the explanation incomplete; the concept of music complexity is also critical here. When listening to it for the first time, it is quite difficult to really appreciate a complex piece such as the ones we often find in the classical music repertoire without having received some training, or education, for this musical style. Indeed, the more complex a piece is, the more time it takes (several repetitions) before being in a position to appreciate it fully. The good news though is that once you like it, it should last longer. It is noteworthy that musical appreciation is tightly associated with emotion and memory. In this context, it is not surprising that different forms of music therapy exist, i.e., therapeutic approaches developed for exploiting the power of evocation of music in clinical psychology.

Curiously enough, some people seem unable to enjoy music when they hear it. This condition is known as *amusia* (Peretz & Hyde, 2003). In general, amusia is a disorder in pitch processing, but for some people, the problem is also related to memory and music recognition deficits. Indeed, congenital amusia and acquired amusia should be distinguished. Approximately 4 % of the population suffer from congenital amusia. These people are born with a kind of deafness to pitch that leads to the inability to recognize or hum a song. That said, the most frequent cause of amusia remains acquired, and its occurrence is due to brain damage.

Finally, among the most noticeable individual differences in music perception, one is quite spectacular: some people are able to identify the specific note that is heard when presented with a sound. They know whether it was a G or a D, for instance, that was presented. The term used to describe this specific quality is *perfect pitch*; these people have perfect pitch.

3.4   Hearing Speech

Because we use language on a daily basis, and likely because we learn and integrate it very early in our life, we tend to take for granted the capacity for understanding and producing language. However, producing the sounds of language and being capable to hear these sounds and extract of them something meaningful are highly sophisticated skills. Speech sounds are often mispronounced for several reasons, including a strong accent from a region or another country or because the person speaking is 3 or 93 years old. Speech sounds can also be pronounced very rapidly or in the context where there is an important background noise; nevertheless, most often we can extract sense.

3.4.1   Linguistic Description

The field of phonetics covers the acoustical study of speech sounds. Each language contains a certain number of basic useful units for communicating. These units are called phonemes. A phoneme is an abstract unit, a speech segment which in itself has no meaning but contributes with other phonemes to generating meaningful sounds. It is neither a letter nor a syllable. Each language counts a certain number of phonemes, but it is difficult to quantify precisely the exact number. For instance, it is often reported that there are 36 phonemes in French, but some authors rather report that there are close to 40 considering the regional disparities in the way of pronouncing sounds. A total of 44 phonemes are reported for English, if diphthongs are included in the count.

The way of pronouncing sounds does not always correspond to the way of spelling them. Consequently, there is a particular way to make a written report of phonemes that is referred to as the International Phonetic Alphabet. This notation was

Table 3.1 Thirty-six phonemes of French language (from *Le Petit Larousse illustré* 2011)

Voyelles	Consonnes	Semi-voyelles (ou semi-consonnes)
Voyelles orales		
[i] *i* (hab*i*t)	[p] *p* (*p*as)	[j] *y* (l*i*eu)
[e] *é* (th*é*)	[t] t (*l*utte)	[ɥ] *u* (l*u*i)
[ɛ] *è* (proc*è*s)	[k] *c, k, qu* (*k*épi)	[w] *ou* (*ou*i)
[a] *a* (*a*voir)	[b] *b* (*b*eau)	
[ɑ] *a* (*â*ne)	[d] *d* (*d*os)	
[ɔ] *o* (r*o*be)	[g] *g* (*g*are)	
[o] *o*(d*o*s)	[f] *f* (*f*ou)	
[u] *ou* (*ou*vrir)	[v] *v* (*v*ite)	
[y] *u* (*u*ser)	[s] *s* (cha*s*se)	
[ø] *eu* (f*eu*)	[z] *z, s* (rai*s*on)	
[œ] *eu* (p*eu*r)	[ʃ] *ch* (*ch*eval)	
[ə] *e* (l*e*)	[ʒ] *j, g* (*j*ambe)	
	[l] *l* (*l*arge)	
Voyelles nasales	[r] *r* (*r*ude)	
[ɛ̃] *in* (p*ain*)	[m] *m* (*m*aison)	
[œ̃] *un* (parf*um*)	[n] *n* (*n*ourrir)	
[ɑ̃] *an, en* (bl*an*c)	[ɲ] *gn* (a*gn*eau)	
[ɔ̃] *on* (b*on*)		

devised by the International Phonetic Association. By convention, the words transcribed in phonetic are placed within brackets and phonemes are presented within slashes. Phonemes of the French language are presented with the phonetic alphabet in Table 3.1 and in Table 3.2 for English language. Although six written vowels (A, E, I, O, U, Y) exist for French and English, there exist 16 phonetic vowels in French and 20 in English. Note that both French and English, for instance, also use phoneme coming from foreign languages (for instance, the "j" in Spanish).

It is on the basis of phonemes in a language that all words in that language can be built. Thus, it becomes possible to generate all words of English language with 44 sounds, phonemes, due to the sole combination between them. There exist hundreds of other phonemes in other languages (for instance, there are 77 phonemes in Lithuanian), but they are not useful for describing words in English. Also, some distinctions like the one between /l/ and /r/, so useful in English or French, will not be helpful in Japanese. In other words, Japanese people might not be able to distinguish "fried rice" from "flied lice."

It is also useful to know that words can be divided on the basis of the units of sense they are made of. These units are called morphemes. There is only one morpheme in a word like "accept," but "unacceptable" includes three morphemes: un-accept-able. Morphemes are reported to be free if they can constitute a word, as is the case for "accept" but are linked if they do not form a word by themselves, as is the case for the "un" of unacceptable.

Table 3.2 Common phonemes of the English language (from John and Sarah Free Materials 1996)

Iː	I	ʊ	uː	Iə	eI	John & Sarah Free Materials 1996
READ	SIT	BOOK	TOO	HERE	DAY	
e	ə	3ː	ɔː	ʊə	ɔI	əʊ
MEN	AMERICA	WORD	SORT	TOUR	BOY	GO
æ	ʌ	ɑː	ɒ	eə	ɑI	ɑʊ
CAT	BUT	PART	NOT	WEAR	MY	HOW
p	b	t	d	tʃ	dʒ	k	g
PIG	BED	TIME	DO	CHURCH	JUDGE	KILO	GO
f	v	θ	ð	s	z	ʃ	ʒ
FIVE	VERY	THINK	THE	SIX	ZOO	SHORT	CASUAL
m	n	ŋ	h	l	r	w	j
MILK	NO	SING	HELLO	LIVE	READ	WINDOW	YES

3.4.2 Technical Analysis

Sounds of language are produced by the passage of air in the nasal cavity, in the mouth, and in the throat and by the work of the tongue and lips. An open respiratory channel leads to the production of vowels, whereas closing movements are associated with the production of consonants. Indeed, there are three characteristics for distinguishing the types of consonants. Consonants differ as a function of the place of articulation, the way of expulsing air, and the level of vibration (voicing) of the vocal cords. The place of articulation is reported to be, for instance, labial (pronounce /b/), dental (pronounce /d/), or labiodental (pronounce /v/). The way of expulsing air can be slow, as is the case with fricatives (pronounce /f/), or sudden, as is the case with occlusives (pronounce /b/ or /t/). Finally, a consonant can generate a large amount of vibration of the vocal cord (voiced consonant as in pronouncing /b/ or /z/) or not much vibration (unvoiced consonant as in pronouncing /f/ and /s/).

It is possible to make an accurate analysis of the frequencies that compose speech sounds by means of a spectrogram. The spectrogram makes it possible to analyze, over a short but continuous period, the contribution of different frequencies in speech sounds. On a spectrogram like the one illustrated in Fig. 3.7, the intensity of various frequencies is presented on the y-axis as a function of time, on the x-axis. Horizontal dark bands in this figure are called formants and are produced during the pronunciation of the letter /a/. In the figure, the first formants are lower and correspond to low frequencies.

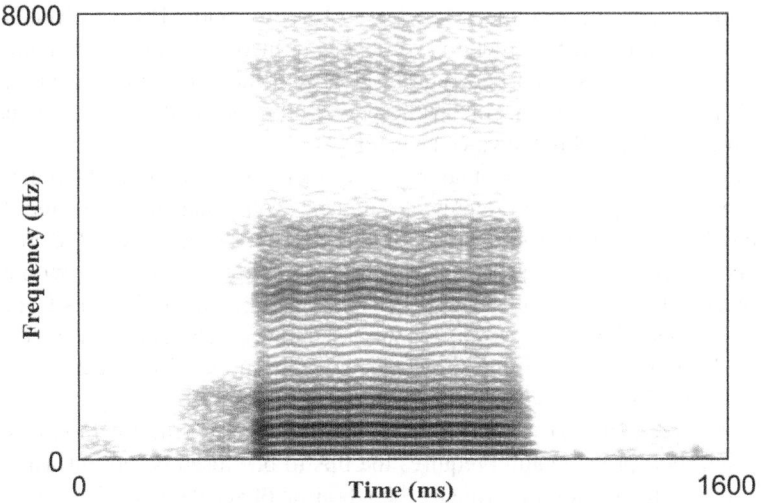

Fig. 3.7 Spectrogram of letter /a/ pronounced during 700 ms

3.4.3   Theoretical Perspectives

Just listening to someone speaking a normal rate of speech, but in a foreign language, is sufficient for getting the impression that the flow of words is continuous.
If you ever had the occasion to learn a second language, you probably remember
how much easier it was to understand when people were kind enough to speak
slowly. The difficulty occurs at the moment of segmenting all spoken sounds, seem-
ingly continuous, into significant units in order to identify words. Even within your
own language, it may happen that you will experience this difficulty, either because
a child is mispronouncing a few words or because you are talking with an elderly
having a very strong regional accent. Indeed, the fundamental question emerging is
the following one: how is it possible to recognize words and understand the message
they carry when there is no clear interruption in the spectrograms corresponding to
these words?

It is tempting to attribute this capacity to the fact that there exists a mechanism
in the brain dedicated to the processing of spoken information. Some researchers
adopt this position, a modular perspective, where the central hypothesis is the
existence of neural circuits specifically for processing speech. On the contrary,
other researchers rather believe in the idea that there is nothing special in the processing of speech sounds; the mechanisms responsible for this processing are the
same as those involved in the processing of other auditory stimuli (Diehl, Lotto,
& Holt, 2004).

More than 50 years ago, an interesting idea was developed according to which it
would be possible to perceive speech because we can produce it. As is the case for
the production of sounds, the motor system would operate in the perception and

recognition of speech (Galantucci, Fowler, & Turvey, 2006). This involvement of the motor system in speech perception would occur unconsciously or automatically. This motor theory of speech perception belongs to the perspective according to which there is something specific with speech processing: there is a language-specific process, located in the voice channel.

This idea is certainly less popular, but other theories based on the modular perspective have been proposed. Sounds of language would actually be distinct from other sounds considering that the perception of it is indeed categorical. We are talking about categorical perception when the discrimination of elements within the same category is more difficult to do than the discrimination of elements from different categories. Therefore, certain sounds of language belonging to a same category, like different forms of a same phoneme, would be more difficult to discriminate than members of different categories like /b/ and /p/.

These two phonemes nevertheless look like each other for different reasons like the fact that their pronunciation requires the lips to be closed before releasing air. Moreover, both phonemes are based on the vibration of vocal chords. However, this vibration does not occur at the same moment in each case. While vibrations occur rapidly when air is released for the pronunciation of /b/, the ones needed for pronouncing /p/ occur only after 50 or 60 ms. This delay before the beginning of vibrations is called *voice onset time*.

Suppose now that this voice onset time is manipulated experimentally with synthetic sounds. For instance, participants are asked to say whether they hear "ba" or "pa." When the voice onset time lasts less than 25 ms, participants report hearing "ba"; however, for voice onset time longer than 35 ms, they report hearing "pa" (Eimas & Corbit, 1973). Between 25 and 35 ms, there is a phonetic frontier where the sounds cannot be distinguished.

When this categorical perception of speech sounds was discovered, it was interpreted as a demonstration of the existence of language-specific neural mechanisms. However, it eventually turned out that nonverbal sounds were also subjects to categorical perception. What is more, nonhuman animals, which are not really competent in spoken language, would also show some form of categorical perception for sound signals (Kluender, Diehl, & Killeen, 1987; Tsunada, Lee, & Cohen, 2011).

The fact that brain areas that are not part of the auditory cortex contribute to language processing can be interpreted like supporting the idea that there are speech specificity mechanisms. In addition to the potential left hemisphere specialization of the brain for language, there are also areas dedicated to the production and to the comprehension of language. For instance, damage to Broca's area located in the lower part of the frontal lobe impairs the capacity to produce speech (Broca's aphasia). Damage to Wernicke's area, in the upper part of the temporal lobe, causes difficulty with language comprehension. Therefore, it is possible for someone to have an intact auditory system, i.e., presenting no sign of difficulty for processing nonlinguistic auditory signals, but still suffering from aphasia.

3.4.4   Intermodality

Of course, oral communication depends on the capacity of producing speech sounds and of detecting and decoding them. Nevertheless, understanding speech goes beyond the sole processing of auditory processing. A powerful demonstration of this fact was reported by McGurk and MacDonald (1976). The McGurk effect, as it is called now, shows the influence exerted by visual signals on the processing of language. Thus, if a participant is shown, with a special experimental device, a speaker saying "ba ba" but with lips pronouncing "ga ga," this participant will likely hear neither "ba" nor "ga," but "da" instead.

Trying to extract the words from a song is a classical case for experiencing difficulties to understand spoken language (this is especially magnified if the song is in a foreign language). These difficulties sometimes lead to a phenomenon called a *mondegreen*[3]: not only is it difficult to understand the lyrics, but one may even hear something different. Lyrics are indeed a most relevant avenue for benefiting from additional visual information for increasing understanding. Jesse and Massaro (2010) tested whether the fact of seeing someone signing, instead of simply seeing someone talking, would help understand lyrics in a song. They showed that recognition could be increased by 35 % compared with conditions where it was possible only to see or to hear the singer.

The fact we can observe such a phenomenon for spoken language and singing language indicates that both domains are linked somehow. Indeed, seeing the face of a singer would influence music perception (Thompson, Russo, & Livingstone, 2010). More particularly, the singer's facial expression would contain information about another aspect of auditory processing, namely, the relations between pitches. In brief, beyond the question of knowing whether processing language is based on specific mechanisms, the question concerning the extent to which speech and language share common characteristics remains most relevant (Patel, 2008).

---

[3] This term comes from a Scottish ballad, "The Bonnie Earl O'Moray", where "And laid him on the green" might well sound like "And Lady *Mondegreen*."

Chapter 4
Biological Bases of Visual Perception

This is the first of a series of chapters on the study of visual perception. Because visual perception has been studied for a long time and because it is easier to illustrate visual phenomena in a book than illustrating phenomena involving any other sensory modality, visual perception has traditionally taken a lot of space in textbooks dedicated to the psychology of perception. The importance of vision in the study of perception may also be explained by the obvious place that this sense occupies in everyday life in humans. This chapter is dedicated to the description of the main biological structures and of some of the mechanisms associated with visual perception.

4.1 The Eye

The eye, which is almost spherical and has a diameter of 2–2.5 cm, is a set of structures which allows the transformation of the light into a code that the brain can understand.

4.1.1 The Eyeball

Figure 4.1 shows the main parts of the eyeball. In its front part, there are ligaments, which hold the lens, and the iris, which is controlling the amount of light entering in the eye. In fact, it is the color of the iris that determines the fact of having, for example, brown or blue eyes. With a diameter ranging from 2 to 8 mm and located in the center of the iris, the pupil lets in more or less light, depending on the fact that it is dilated or contracted. One can easily see the direct effect of light on the state of the iris and pupil. Just look at someone in the eyes in the dark and then turn on a light. You will see a reflex activity, called the Whytt reflex, in which the pupil diameter gradually decreases.

© Springer International Publishing Switzerland 2016
S. Grondin, *Psychology of Perception*, DOI 10.1007/978-3-319-31791-5_4

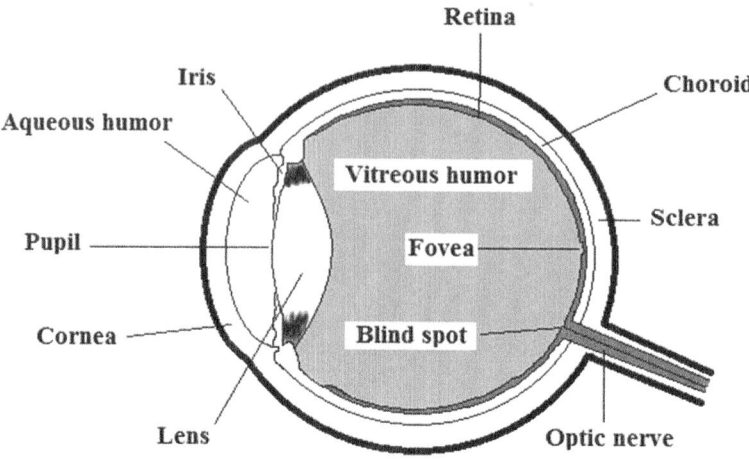

Fig. 4.1 Main structures of the eye

The light rays entering the eye are first bent by a curved membrane, the cornea, before crossing the pupil where they are bent again. Another adjustment of rays is done through an automatic mechanism called accommodation, which consists of a more or less pronounced flattening of the lens. The lens becomes rather round if the object on which we try to focus on is close or very flat if the object is far. Thus, if an object is near, the muscles contract; the lens becomes thicker and the light rays are bent even more.

The outermost part of the eye is the sclera. The sclera is resistant and maintains the shape of the eye. In its anterior part, it is transparent and covered by a thin membrane, the conjunctiva, which has a protecting role. Between the sclera and the retina, there is an intermediate membrane, the choroid, or choroid membrane, which allows to avoid the presence of light reflection (internal) by absorbing light. Highly vascularized, the choroid has a nutritive function for retinal cells.

Note that the spherical shape of the eye is made possible by the presence of two types of fluid. In the anterior part, between the cornea and the lens, this fluid is called the aqueous humor. In the back part, there is a large space filled with a rather gelatinous substance called the vitreous humor.

In the posterior part of the eye, there is a blind spot (or optic disk) caused by the presence of the optic nerve. This spot covers approximately 7.5° on the vertical axis and 5° on the horizontal axis (approximately 2.1 mm × 1.5 mm). The brain manages to compensate for the loss of vision caused by the blind spot (Fig. 4.2).

The innermost layer of the eye's posterior part is the retina. It is on the retina that the image is formed. Given its importance in vision, the next subsection is devoted to it. On the retina is a point having a diameter of about 1°, the fovea. It is at the fovea that we have the sharpest vision. The fovea is located 2 mm from the blind spot in a small area, the macula lutea (or yellow spot). In this area, there is a high concentration of cones. In fact, at the center of the fovea, there are only cones.

Fig. 4.2 Demonstration about the presence of the blind spot. (1) You need to fixate X on the *top row* with your right eye, keeping the left eye closed. From the corner of your eye, you should still be able to see the *black disk* located on the same row. Then, with a movement of your arm that is holding the book, you will vary the distance between your eye and the X. At a given distance, the visible *black disk* in the corner of your eye should disappear, although it is possible to see it a little further or a little closer. (2) You should repeat the demonstration with the *bottom row*. This time, if you fixate X, you should, at a given distance, perceive a non-interrupted *black line*; this interruption, in *white*, should disappear, the brain having compensate the loss of vision caused by the presence of the *black spot*

Finally, each eyeball is provided with three pairs of muscles that direct the eye in all directions of the visual field. These pairs have actually antagonistic roles. The superior and inferior lower rectus muscles allow the eye to make movements in the vertical direction, from top to bottom and from bottom to top; the lateral and medial rectus muscles make possible the horizontal movements, to the left or to the right; and the inferior (which is smaller) and superior (which is larger) oblique muscles are responsible for torsional movements and are involved in the vertical movements.

4.1.2 The Retina

The retina covers a section of about 200° in the posterior part of the eye and has a surface of about 25 cm^2 and a thickness of about 4 mm. As illustrated in Fig. 4.3, the retina is made essentially of three layers of cells. There are photoreceptor cells, which convert the electromagnetic energy (light) into nerve impulses. This information is transmitted to higher centers through the other two layers: the bipolar and ganglion cells. The retina is also made of horizontal and amacrine cells whose function is to facilitate the transfer of information between neurons of the same level.

There are two types of photoreceptor cells in the retina, the rods and the cones, which have different functions and properties. These types of cells do not have the same sensitivity to light. There are about five million cones and 120 million rods. Because of their high response threshold, the cones are assigned to daytime vision and form the photopic system. The cones are responsive to color and provide better visual acuity than the rods. We find a very large concentration of cones—about 35,000—at the fovea.

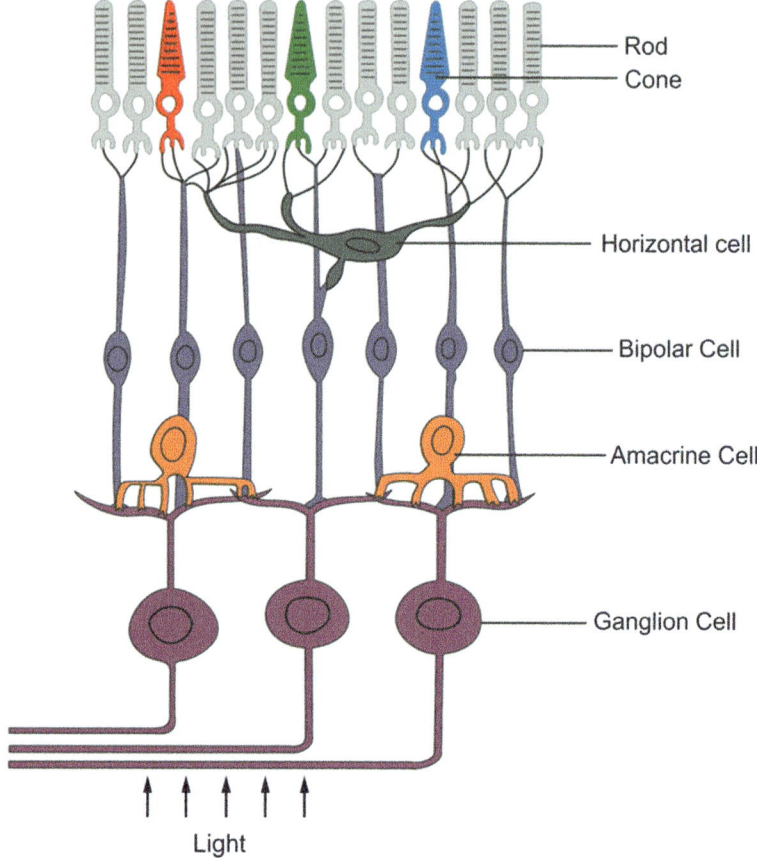

Rod

Cone

Horizontal cell

Bipolar Cell

Amacrine Cell

Ganglion Cell

Light

Fig. 4.3 Layers of retinal cells (figure by Leila Aazari)

For their part, the rods are more elongated than cones. Sensitive to low light intensity, the rods are assigned to night vision (the scotopic system). Moving away from fovea to periphery, the rods are more and more numerous, and, unlike the cones, their shape remains almost always the same.

The rods and cones are made of photosensitive pigments. The pigments of the cones are of three types in that the absorption of light of each of these types is maximal at certain wavelengths, long, medium, and short (see Chap. 5 on color perception). The photosensitive pigment of rods, rhodopsin, absorbs wavelengths ranging from 400 to 600 nm. It is therefore a photochemical process that will create an action potential which will be transmitted from the retina to the brain.

Bipolar cells, which can take different forms and different sizes, are involved in the passage of nerve impulses from the photoreceptors to the ganglion cells. Bipolar cells synapse with both rods with cones. Depending on whether it is located at periphery or at the fovea, the number of receptors in contact with the bipolar cells varies. Thus, the bipolar cells of the fovea may receive impulses from only one cone, while a little further at periphery, they may receive information from several photoreceptors. In general, bipolar cells specific to the cones are in contact with less photoreceptors than bipolar cells receiving information from rods. Moreover, the photoreceptors are in contact with each other through the horizontal cells. Some are only in contact with cones, others only with rods; other cells may be in contact with these two types of photoreceptors. These horizontal cells can also synapse with bipolar cells. The reader will find in DeValois and DeValois (1988) additional information about the connections between photoreceptors, horizontal cells, and bipolar cells and about the biological mechanisms underlying vision.

Bipolar cells mainly transmit nerve impulses to the ganglion cells, but also to amacrine cells. The role of the latter is comparable to that of the horizontal cells in that they mainly assume a role of interaction, this time between the ganglion and bipolar cells. For their part, the ganglion cells receive impulses mainly from of one or more bipolar neurons. The farther we get in periphery, the more frequent are the contributions of bipolar and amacrine cells to the excitement of a ganglion cell. The axons of the ganglion cells eventually form the optic nerve. For each eye, there are about one million ganglion cells.

4.2 Receptive Fields

It is important to understand that the retina has a particular organization as it includes more than 125 million receptors, cones, or rods, but does transmit information to the visual cortex cells through only a million ganglion cells. In fact, this particular arrangement of retinal cells refers to the idea of receptive field. To each ganglion cell corresponds a receptive field, which is a surface at the photoreceptor level where the light causes a change on the normal course of the electrical activity.

Early work in neurophysiology has shown that the light projected on the retina causes three types of responses (Hartline, 1940; Hartline & Ratliff, 1957; Kuffler, 1953). Thus, the response recorded at the ganglion cell level using an electrode can be one of the following three (Fig. 4.4). Cell responses show (1) an increase in activity during stimulation, and, from the beginning of the stimulation, then a return to normal activity when the illumination ceases; (2) an interruption of any activity while the light is on, but an acceleration of these responses when the light is turned off; and (3) an increase in activity at the beginning, followed by a decrease, and the repetition of this pattern (increase-decrease) when the light is off. These three types of responses are respectively called "on," "off," and "on-off."

The responses given by the ganglion cells depend on the stimulated location on the retina. Stimulating the retina at a specific location, or nearby, can result in responses of different types on a given ganglion cell. Indeed, to each ganglion cell corresponds a receptive field. This field could be of two types: on-center or off-center. These two types of field have a circular shape (Fig. 4.5) and are divided in equal number on the retina. For a type of field, stimulation at center causes "on" responses, and around this center, responses are "off." Between these two levels,

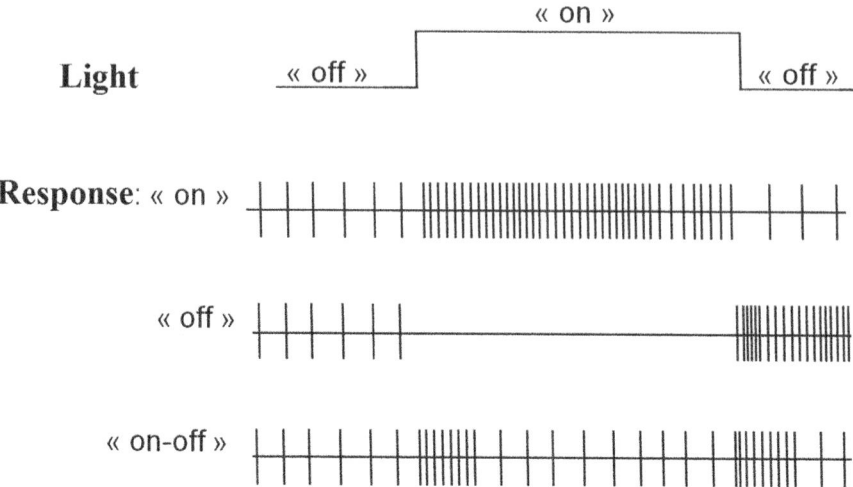

Fig. 4.4 Illustration of activation and inhibition patterns on ganglion cells with the arrival, maintenance, and disappearance of the light stimulation

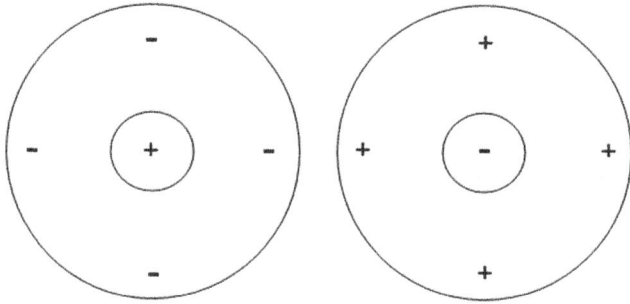

Fig. 4.5 Two types of circular receptive fields: with an "on" *center* (*left*) and with an "off" *center* (*right*)

there are responses of another type, "on-off." For the second type of receptive field, stimulation causes off responses in the center and around this center, on responses. In other words, the ganglion cells are in a position to gather information on the center of their receptive field and on the surrounding region.

In fact, there is critical distinction between two types of ganglion cells: "magno" versus "parvo." About 80% of ganglion cells are of the parvo type (P cells, sometimes called "X"), and the magno cells (M cells or "Y") represent 10% of these ganglion cells. There is also a third class of ganglion cells ("W") which would have a receptive field different of those described above and which would have the slowest conduction speed.

Parvo cells have a small receptive field (diameter of 0.01 mm) and a conduction speed of about 20 m/s. In contrast, magno cells have a larger receptive field. For

	Magno (Y)	Parvo (X)
Represent (of total)	10%	80%
Body cells and axons	Larger	Smaller
Conduction speed	40 m/s	20 m/s
Neural responses	Jerkily	Continuous
Receptive field	Larger	Smaller
Contrast sensitivity	High	Low
Sensitive to	Large objects	Colors
Sensitive to	Movement	Stationary patterns

Table 4.1 Contrasting the characteristics of two types of ganglion cells, magno and parvo

example, at 10 mm from the fovea, the receptive fields are 50 times larger (0.5 mm). Because their body cell and axon are larger, magno cells have a much greater conduction speed (40 m/s) than parvo cells. Table 4.1 summarizes the main features that differentiate these two types of ganglion cells, P and M.

4.3   Central Mechanisms

The grouping of ganglion cell axons forms the optic nerve. The distance between the exit of the eye and the optic chiasm is about 5 cm. At the optic chiasma level, a shift occurs in the routing of a part of the information arriving from the eye. As indicated by the word chiasma, there is a crossing of information. Approximately 50% of the information from one eye is transferred to the opposite side of the brain. It is the information received in the nasal portion of the retina (the part of the retina closest to the nose) that is intersecting at the optic chiasm level. The fibers from the temporal region of the retina remain on the same side. Whether the optic nerve fibers cross or not, there is no synapse at the optic chiasm location. Also, beyond the optic chiasm, the optic nerve is called the optic tract.

The information carried by each optical track therefore comes from each eye and is directed to one of the following two structures, the lateral geniculate nucleus (LGN) and the superior colliculus, most of the visual information being routed to the LGN. The superior colliculi, which are a primitive structure of the brain, have no role in the detection of the exact nature of the stimuli, but would be used to locate their source. The superior colliculi also exert control on the movement of the eyes when they should be moved to look at an object in periphery.

As for the LGN, this structure has a much greater contribution to the whole visual processing. As the name suggests, they are located on each side of the brain and have the shape of a flexed knee. Each of the LGN, the left and right, has a receptive field similar to that of ganglion cells. They also have a retinotopic organization, that is to say, that the representation on the retina is maintained at the LGN level. The other features of the LGN include the fact that they are made up of six separate layers that do receive information from only one eye, that they have a key role in the perception of form, and, more than the superior colliculi, that they receive a lot of information from the fovea. Consequently, the LGN are involved in the perception of color.

4.3.1   The Visual Cortex

The visual cortex is located in the occipital part of the brain and has an area of approximately 64 cm^2. The cerebral organization in the brain also preserves the spatial organization of retinal cells (retinotopic organization), but the amount of space occupied in the brain depends on the location stimulated on the retina. About 65 % of the visual cortex is associated with the activity on the retina corresponding to 10 % of the visual field.

The terms V1–V5 are now used for describing the different regions of the visual cortex, and two main sections should also be kept in mind, the primary visual cortex and the secondary visual cortex (Table 4.2). The primary visual cortex, or striate cortex, is also sometimes called area 17. This corresponds to the visual 1 (V1) area. The V1 area receives information from LGN, which also has a spatial arrangement corresponding to a retinotopic organization. The V1 area is divided into six layers designated by the numbers 1–6. The information from the LGN arrives at the fourth layer (specifically 4c) in V1.

The second section, the secondary visual cortex or extrastriate cortex, includes areas V2 and V3 (or area 18) and V4 and V5 (or area 19). It is in these areas that are routed nerve impulses coming from superior colliculi. Similarly, some information already processed in V1 will reach certain areas of the secondary visual cortex. Finally, the processing of visual information also involves the contribution of another part of the visual cortex called the associative cortex. It is in this part of the visual cortex that some learning and some past associations intervene in the overall perception.

Some other features of the visual cortex are noteworthy. The knowledge of these features relies essentially on the pioneer work of two neurobiologists, David Hubel and Torsten Wiesel, who won the Nobel Prize in Physiology in 1981 (Hubel & Wiesel, 1959, 1962). Essentially, Hubel and Wiesel used a technique allowing the recording of the activity of one cell at a time in the visual cortex. They found that the receptive fields in the visual cortex are not necessarily circular. For example, they are sometimes elongated. They identified three types of cells in the visual cortex to which they gave the name of simple cells, complex cells, and hypercomplex cells.

Table 4.2 Names given to areas in the primary and secondary visual cortex

	Primary visual cortex	Secondary visual cortex
Other name	Striate visual cortex	Extrastriate visual cortex
Brodmann classification	Area 17	Areas 18 and 19
Common nomenclature	Area V1	Areas V2, V3, V4, and V5

The response of simple cells is maximal when an observer is presented with a specific orientation. Simple cells in layer 4c of the area V1 have for their part a circular receptive field. The selectivity for orientation (bars placed more or less vertically or horizontally) is a fundamental feature of these simple cells. A change of a few degrees of a bar significantly reduces the electrical activity, or neural response made by a given cell, but increases the activity of another of these simple cells located in V1.

Because it is more difficult to know what determines their activity, a second type of cells is called "complex cells." They are found in the layers 2, 3, 5, and 6 of V1. It is known that they are sensitive to movement, some to movement in one direction, the others to movement in another direction. In brief, we are referring here to a case of selectivity for motion perception.

Even more difficult to understand, the hypercomplex cells appear to be end-stopped cells. They respond only to edges having a specific orientation or moving in a certain direction.

In their work, Hubel and Wiesel also identified an important feature of the organization of cells in V1. The visual cortex is built with architecture in columns. Thus, when inserting an electrode vertically, beginning from layer 1 up to the layer 6, it is always the bars of the same orientation that give maximal responses. That sequence of six layers is called a column. When moving the electrode on a horizontal plane, there is a gradual change about the cell preference to stimuli ranging from horizontal to vertical: this sequence of columns are called hypercolumn and have an area of about 2 mm^2. There are about 6400 hypercolumns composed of 15,000 cells each.

There are in the brain several specialized processing areas for specific functions or features. In other words, there is a segregation of the various functions related to visual processing and an assignment of these functions to specific areas in the visual cortex. Areas V1 and V2 are alike as they both have small receptive fields and form, according to some authors, a V1–V2 complex. In addition to the characteristics described above, it should be noted that in V1, the segregation applies according to shape, color, and movement. Area V2 receives some information directly from the LGN but mostly receives information via relays from V1.

Area V3 is very closely linked to the activity at the fovea and is specialized in the processing of form. This area however would also contain information about the position changes of the form or object. Area V4 is specialized in the processing of color, more specifically in the processing of reflected light. Area V5 processes movement; more specifically, most of the cells in this area would respond to movement in a particular direction.

4.3.2 Visual Pathways

We distinguish two major pathways in the processing of visual information. Their name refers to the origin of the stimulation and where it ends up. Thus, the first pathway is called magnoparietal. It is also referred to as the median temporal pathway or dorsal pathway (or even *geniculostriate*). This pathway provides information about the "where" and "how" aspects of vision and requires the contribution of

10% of ganglion cells. As this pathway passes through V5, it is not surprising that it is associated with motion perception.

The other pathway is called parvotemporal or ventral (*tectopulvinar*). It is also known as the "what" pathway. This pathway requires the contribution of areas V2 and V4, the latter indicating that it involves color processing. In fact, this pathway allows to scrutinize images or objects for identifying them correctly.

Finally, this chapter on the biological bases of visual perception would be incomplete without the presentation of some principles. For example, relatively to a fixation point straight ahead, what is located on the left will be processed in the right cerebral hemisphere, and what is located on the right will be processed in the left hemisphere. Figure 4.6 illustrates in what position the information captured from

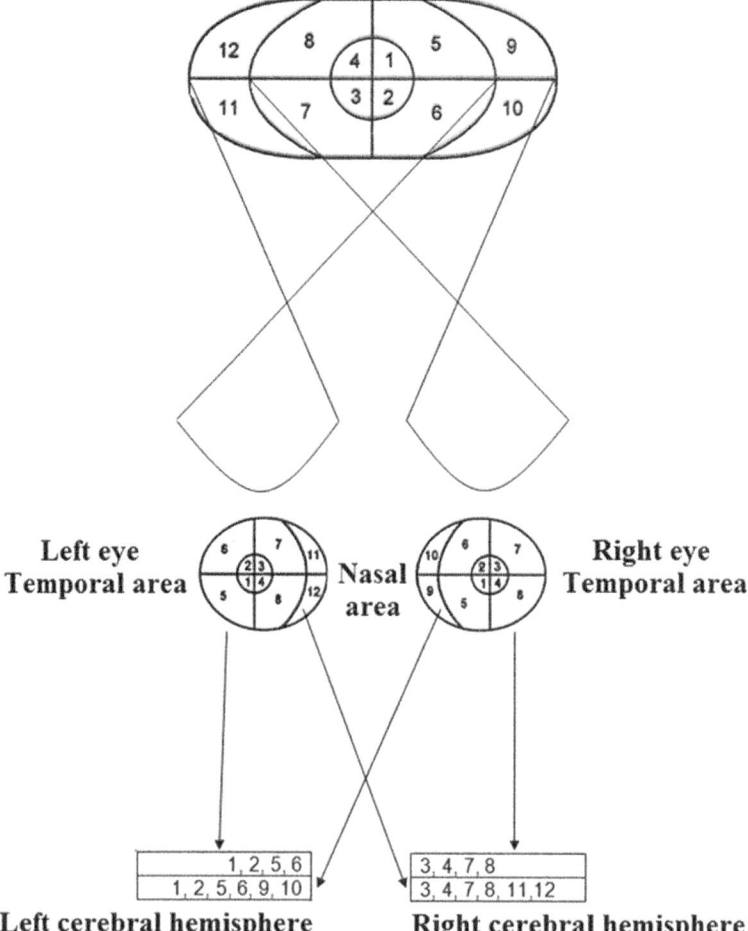

Fig. 4.6 In relation to the visual field, each eye receives information that is upside down and mirrored; also, what is located to the right of the fixation point arrives in the left cerebral hemisphere, and what is located to the left of the fixation point arrives in the right cerebral hemisphere

the visual field arrives on the retina and in the cerebral hemispheres. Thus, it is possible to observe that, relative to the visual field, the image on the retina is upside down and mirrored. Also, the properties of the optic chiasm lead to (1) the passage of information from the nasal region of the left eye (information contained in the left side of the visual field) to the right side of the brain and (2) the passage of information from the nasal region of the right eye (information contained on the right side of the visual field) to the left side of the brain. This crossover explains why each cerebral hemisphere is responsible for processing the visual information presented to the opposite side.

4.4 Clinical Aspects

Different problems may arise that will impede the proper functioning of the visual system. We can distinguish various categories of disorders that lead to poorer vision. The most common are listed here. Color vision disorders are presented in the following chapter.

A first major category of problems, and the most frequent indeed, is related to the capacity of focusing. Refraction problems (or refractive errors) prevent the light rays to reach the retina so that the picture is clear. One type of refraction problem is called *hypermetropia*. This occurs when the distance between the lens and the retina is too short (Fig. 4.7). The image is formed behind the fovea. The person suffering from hypermetropia will have difficulty to see near objects. Glasses with a biconvex lens allow to correcting this problem.

Conversely, a person suffers from *myopia* when the distance between the lens and the retina is too large; the image is formed in front of the fovea. Sometimes, a distinction is made between refractive myopia, which means that the light rays are too deflected by the cornea or by the lens, and axial myopia, which means that the eyeball is too long. The person suffering from myopia, or nearsighted, does not see clearly distant objects and will benefit from the use of biconcave lenses. This very common problem can be corrected by photorefractive keratectomy. This is a laser surgery for changing the curvature of the cornea. After the operation, the light rays reach the retina correctly and vision is in focus.

There are rarer cases where a person suffers from *astigmatism*, which means that this person does not have clear vision in all directions of the visual field. A part of the visual field always remains out of focus. This is caused by a nonspherical curvature of the cornea or lens.

Furthermore, *presbyopia* refers to a difficulty to focus on an object that is nearby and is caused by the hardening of the lens with age. It is common that people in their forties, who until then had never experienced any vision problem whatsoever, may need glasses. You may have noted that, without their glasses, older people tend to hold a book at arm's length for reading it. The reduction of the lens' plasticity eventually makes reading much more difficult.

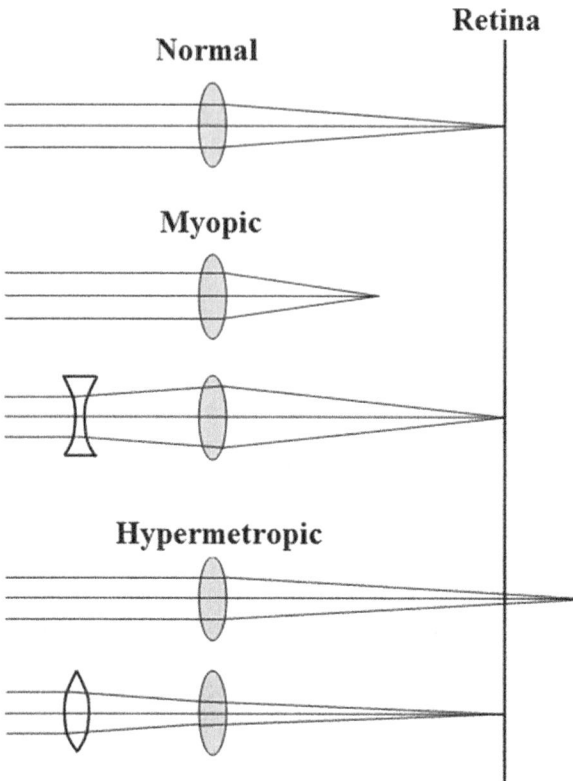

Fig. 4.7 Refraction problems often caused by an anormal shape of the eyeball. After passing through the lens (*gray*), light rays arrive at the retina in front of a myopic eye or behind the hypermetropic eye. Normal view could be recovered with a biconcave lens, for myopia, or a biconvex lens, for hypermetropia

Sometimes, instead of being improperly refracted, the light that enters the eye is rather blurred. This can be caused by certain injuries or diseases. It may happen that the cornea is infected, causing vision problems. Furthermore, there are various cases of *cataract*, which refers to the opacity of the lens. The gradual loss of lens transparency in some cases may cause a loss of vision. Cataracts may be congenital or caused by disease (secondary cataract) or injuries (traumatic cataracts). Most often, cataracts are caused by aging. It affects 75 % of people aged 65 and older, and 95 % of those aged 85 and older. Problems caused by cataracts can be corrected with a surgery when the reduction of vision becomes too severe.

Some vision problems are caused by a problem specific to the retina. One such problem is the age-related macular degeneration. With such a problem, a person sees somehow very well everywhere except where he or she is looking, i.e., where the focus is made! There are also cases of retinopathy caused by diabetes. Problems often develop after several years of diabetes. Older people who have long suffered from diabetes can have serious vision problems. Also, poor vision may result from a poor flow of information at the optic nerve; this problem might be caused by an intoxication or inflammation. Finally, vision can be disrupted by a displacement of the retina. In addition, certain injuries can cause a retinal detachment and impair severely sometimes peripheral vision, sometimes central vision.

Another group of eye problems is *glaucoma*. This is a common cause of blindness. Glaucoma is a degeneration of optic nerve sometimes caused by a very large pressure within the eye. Glaucoma usually occurs in people aged over 60 years.

Note in conclusion that there are many other problems that can affect vision. Some of these are related to muscles. That is the case of *strabismus*, which consists of a poor centering of the image (which does not arrive at the fovea) and which causes double vision. It is caused by a disorder in the extraocular muscles, for example, by a paralysis of the muscles of an eye. *Nystagmus*, which refers to a continuous movement of the eyes, is another problem having of muscular origin, this time due to the presence of plaques in the eyes. Finally, *scotoma* is the name given to visual field defects. These deficits can be more or less important and may affect specific portions of the field. In rare cases, this problem can be caused by a lesion to the visual cortex.

Chapter 5
Color Perception

Colors are everywhere in our lives and we could not imagine life without them. They are useful, if only to inform us about the state of ripeness of a fruit or the status of any other food that we are about to eat. They help in basic tasks such as the detection and discrimination of objects. In addition, and perhaps most importantly, they make life enjoyable. For example, we are sensitive to the color of the walls or clothing and to their arrangement.

Yet, the study of colors long remained a mystery. We will see in this chapter that understanding the perception of colors requires the integration of the basic concepts about the nature of physical stimuli underlying visual sensation and about retinal physiology. These concepts are necessary if we want to understand what the brain must deal with for providing relevant information about what is colored in the environment.

5.1 Description of Light

Each sensory receptor is particularly sensitive to a specific form of stimulation. For example, stimuli may be chemical, as in the case of taste or smell, or mechanical, as in the case of touch. If the ear is sensitive to variations in the air pressure, the eye is for its part sensitive to electromagnetic radiation. Light, which is a particular form of this radiation, produces a visual response. Light can be described either by considering that the irradiated energy is propagated in the form of a continuous wave or by considering that it is composed of specific matter particles, the photons.

© Springer International Publishing Switzerland 2016
S. Grondin, *Psychology of Perception*, DOI 10.1007/978-3-319-31791-5_5

5.1.1 Intensity

Light intensity could be expressed in number of photons, but it is agreed to use different photometric units. The basic unit of photometry is called *candle*. A candle is the standard value of light intensity. For example, with a wavelength of 555 nm, a candle produces an amount of energy slightly above 0.001 W.

For understanding color perception, it is important first to identify the nature of what reaches the eye and to distinguish two types of sensory experiences, the incident light and the reflected light. The amount of energy that comes directly from a light source is the radiance, or luminous flux, whereas the amount of light emanating from that source and reaching a surface is called incident light or illuminance. Meter-candle is the term used to describe the illuminance, and this equals the illumination of a 1-m^2 surface located 1 m away from a standard candle.

The light from a source rarely reaches the eye directly, unless someone looks at this source directly. Most often, the light is reflected from various surfaces in the direction of the eye. This reflected light is called luminance. It is sometimes referred to as surface light. The luminance of a surface is expressed with a unit called candle per square meter (cd/m^2), i.e., the amount of light reflected in all directions by a surface (reflecting and diffusing light perfectly) illuminated by a meter-candle. Because the luminance was once expressed in footlambert or millilambert (mL), one can still find these units in some textbooks. To give a rough idea of the value of different luminances, snow in the sun provides 10^5 cd/m^2; an overcast sky is about 3000 cd/m^2; easy reading requires a luminance of 100 cd/m^2; and the absolute threshold is about 10^{-6} cd/m^2.

The luminance of a surface definitely depends on the incident light and also on another property called reflectance. The reflectance of a surface is its ability to reflect light. Reflectance is expressed with a coefficient. Thus, a surface which has 70 % reflectance reflects 70 % of incident light:

$$\text{reflectance} = \big(\text{luminance} / \text{illuminance}\big) \times 100$$

Sometimes, the concept of retinal illuminance could be useful. This is the amount of light that reaches the retina, and this quantity is expressed in *trolands*.

5.1.2 Wavelength and Spectral Composition

As a whole, the electromagnetic spectrum ranges from 10^{-14} to 10^8 m. This, however, is only the part of the spectrum that is visible. The eye can only perceive wavelengths that lie between 400 and 700 nm (Fig. 5.1). A nanometer is 10^{-9} m. Waves that are a little below 400 nm are called ultraviolet rays; waves above 700 nm are referred to as infrared rays. Although at the physical level the variety of waves ranging from 400 to 700 nm is a continuum, perceptually, the human observer rather

Fig. 5.1 Visible
wavelength in the
electromagnetic spectrum

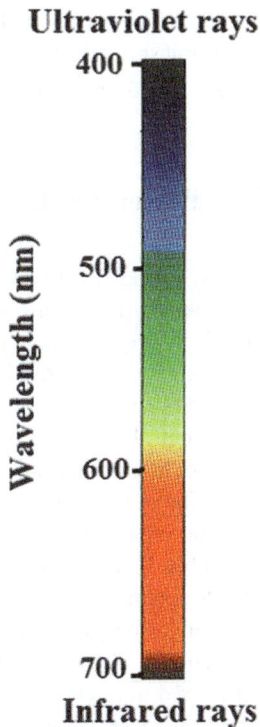

distinguishes color categories. We can distinguish hundreds of colors, but in everyday life, we most often refer only to a few categories. In fact, we will see in the next section to what refers exactly the term color.

It is extremely rare that a light beam contains only one wavelength. Should this happen, it would be called a monochromatic light. Most often, a light beam comprises several wavelengths and thus composes a so-called polychromatic light. All the light energy, however, will not necessarily be distributed equally among all wavelengths. Indeed, different lights vary according to their different spectral compositions. The relative importance of the different waves therefore varies from one light to another.

Between a monochromatic light and a polychromatic light extending over a wide range of waves, there are many possible variations. If a light is monochromatic, it will be reported as being pure. Indeed, the more light is concentrated in a narrow band, the purer it is. In contrast to the purity of the monochromatic light, there may be a case where, for a given beam, all the light energy of all visible wavelengths is distributed into equal proportions. In such a case, we will refer to a white light, and the purity of this light will be null (zero).

To end this section, it is relevant to note that the composition of the light that reaches the eye depends on two factors. Of course, it depends on the spectral composition of the light emitted by a source. It also depends on the properties of a given surface. We refer to reflective properties, in the case of reflected light, or to transmission properties, when light is transmitted through something. In short, two factors determine what reaches to the eye: the emitted light and the properties of a given surface.

5.2 Perceptual Dimensions of Color

What is normally called color most often refers to one of the three basic dimensions that make up the experience of color. This dimension often called "color" is indeed hue. There are chromatic hues (green, yellow, etc.) and achromatic hues. Chromatic hues are determined by the wavelength, but the achromatic hues rather range from white to black, passing through the different shades of gray. In the latter case, their hue is neutral (we can say that there is no hue).

If the different shades of gray do not differ in their hue, how can we distinguish them? The eye can discriminate these grays, and the black and the white, on the basis of the different degrees of lightness. The continuum extends from zero lightness (the case of black) to maximum lightness or almost (the case of white). In between, there is a whole continuum of gray. In the same way that there are different degrees of lightness for distinguishing achromatic stimuli, there are different degrees of lightness for chromatic stimuli. For either chromatic or achromatic hue, it is indeed the term brightness that is used to refer to this concept of lightness or lightness of stimuli. More specifically, brightness will be qualified as light or dark when describing a surface, but when dealing with a light source, the description will be in terms of more or less intense.

In addition to hue and brightness, there is a third perceptual dimension for describing a visual stimulation. This third dimension is called saturation and refers to the degree of purity of light. For example, one can have the impression that a particular green seems to contain more or less green or, in other words, seems to contain more or less gray. When an impression of gray is larger, it is that the light has lost purity. A light that is losing in purity is said to be less and less saturated. On the contrary, if a green, for instance, seems very accentuated or highly concentrated, it means that the saturation level is high.

If a color would contain a lot of gray to the point of losing the impression that there is any color, this would mean that its saturation is null (zero). What would be perceived then would be located somewhere between white and black. Figure 5.2 synthesizes the three fundamental dimensions to be understood to fully grasp what can be experienced with respect to colors.

5.3 Color Mixtures

In order to efficiently describe the experience of color perception, we must integrate the information above about the physical bases of light stimulation, as well as other principles. Thus, it is necessary to understand the concept of primary colors and to distinguish between additive and subtractive color mixtures.

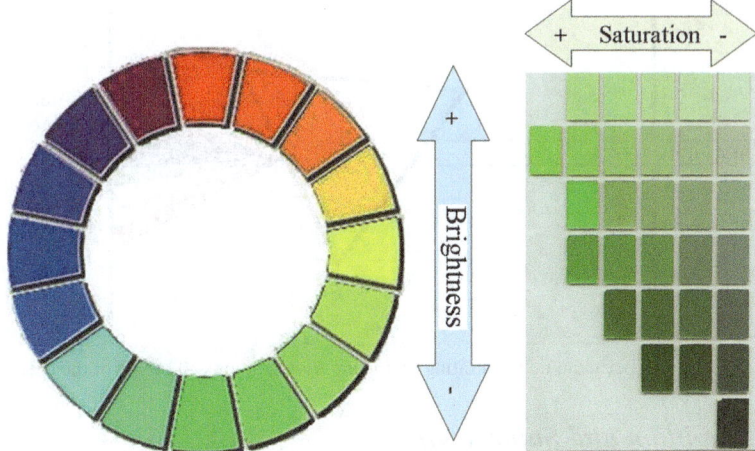

Fig. 5.2 The three basic dimensions at the basis of different shades of colors. The different hues are on the *left*, and the *green squares* on the *right* have different brightness and different saturations

5.3.1   Primary Colors

Despite the adaptive significance of colors in many animal species, and human life in general, it was not until the seventeenth century that new ideas allowed some understanding of the perception of light and color. Until then, the perception of what appeared white to people was interpreted as an absence of color. Intuitively, this naïve interpretation was quite appropriate.

Supported by a simple empirical demonstration, Isaac Newton reported this important idea: the white rather consists of a summation of all colors. His experience consisted of passing beams of white light (sun rays) through a small opening and then through a prism (Fig. 5.3). Beyond the prism, these rays reached a screen. On the screen, these rays did not appeared white anymore, but rather showed the entire color spectrum, the diffraction of the different rays being linked to their wavelength. Newton completed his argument by adding, reversed, a second prism which had the effect of recomposing white light. This demonstration led Newton to conclude that all colors, that is to say, all the wavelengths, were contained in the white light. Newton also advanced another great principle of color perception: to any color corresponds a second color which, mixed with the first, leads to white. These colors are called complementary colors.

Another great idea would later advance our understanding of color perception: there are primary colors, and there are three such primary colors. Primary colors are colors whose combination allows the production of white and the whole range of other colors. Many combinations of colors may constitute the three primary colors. The key point is to select three colors where the mixture of two of them cannot produce the third. On the basis of an arbitrary decision of the *Commission internationale de l'éclairage* (CIE), the three primary colors are defined as blue (435.8 nm), green (546.1 nm), and red (700 nm).

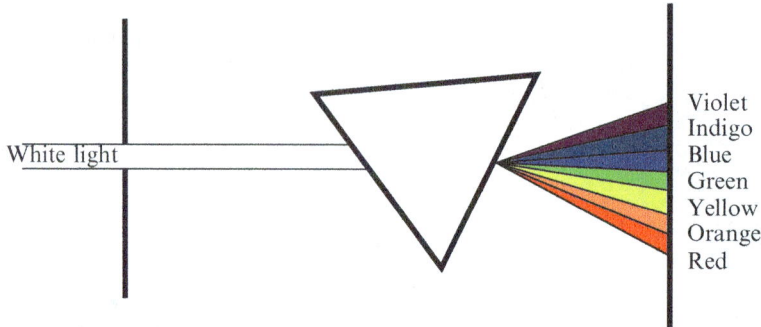

Fig. 5.3 Newton's experiment demonstrating that *white light* contains all colors of the spectrum

5.3.2   Addition and Subtraction

These different concepts relative to light and color are somewhat counterintuitive in that they fail to explain certain phenomena observed in everyday life. For example, working with crayons, each child has experienced the emergence of the green when blue and yellow were mixed. This observation leads some children to believe, wrongly, that yellow, but not green, is a primary color because green would result from a mixture. However, the mixture of two light beams projected on a same location, one that would previously been passed through a yellow filter and the other through a blue filter, will not permit to obtain green. Understanding the difference in the results obtained with crayons and with light beams requires distinguishing between the following two basic concepts: the additive mixtures and the subtractive mixtures.

Common experiences are examples of subtractive mixtures. They are based on the mixture of pigments, that is to say, on the fact that different objects contain a substance which absorbs certain wavelengths and reflects others. Thus, the color of objects does not depend on the properties of light, but rather on how pigments respond to light. In other words, an additive mixture is based on the addition of wavelengths, while a subtractive mixture prevents certain wavelengths to contribute in the color of an object. This impediment is caused by the presence, in this object, of pigments which absorb certain wavelengths. These absorbed waves cannot be reflected and, by extension, will not reach the eye and will not be perceived. With an additive mixture of colors, the resulting color will be brighter than each of the colors used in the mixture; in contrast, a subtractive mixture will result in a decrease of the brightness compared to each of the colors used. Figure 5.4 illustrates the concepts of subtractive and additive mixtures.

It is possible to predict the addition of certain colors on the basis of certain rules. The understanding of these rules is facilitated by observing the color circle shown in Fig. 5.5. This circle illustrates two subjective dimensions of color: (1) the circumference means the hue and (2) the radius designates the saturation. The circumference covers all wavelengths of the visible spectrum from violet (about 400 nm) to

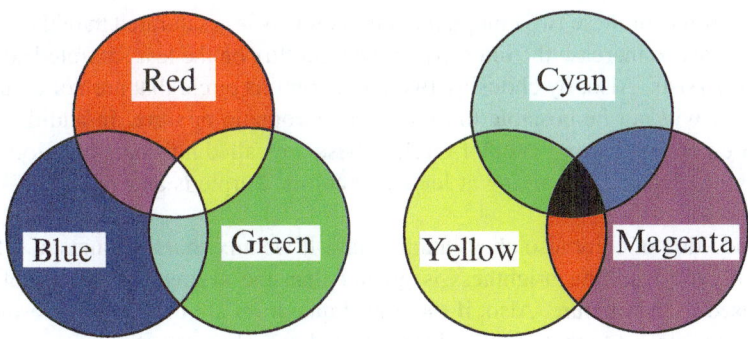

Fig. 5.4 Illustration of the resulting color from an additive (*left*) or subtractive (*right*) mixture

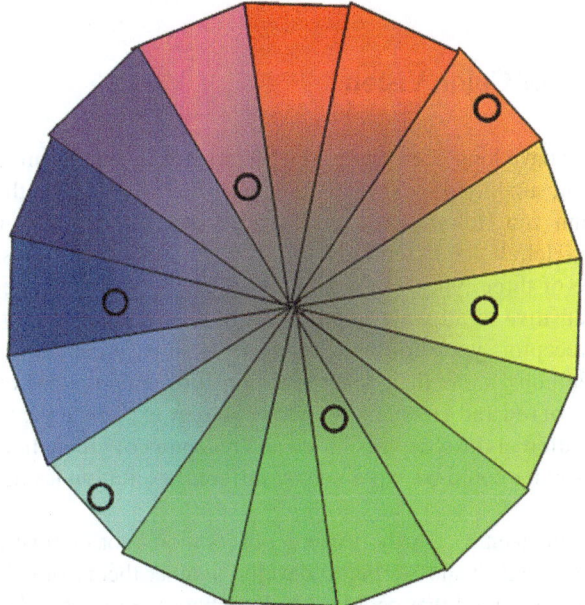

Fig. 5.5 Illustration with the *color wheel* of the resulting additive mixture. For a given pair of points diametrically in opposition, if one provides the same amount of intensity on each side, the resulting mixture is a point in the middle, i.e., some *gray* or *white*

red (about 700 nm). Also, the further away we get from the center of the circle, the greater the saturation is. The center corresponds to a zero degree of saturation, i.e., gray or even to white if the brightness is high.

On this circle, the complementary colors are diametrically opposed. Also, the closer we get to the center, the less saturated they are. If we take two equal amounts of light energy associated with two complementary colors which are located at equal distances from the center, then the resulting mixture gives white (or gray).

However, if one of these two complementary colors is less saturated than the other, it is necessary to increase the intensity of the light flux on the less saturated so that no color persists. Also, by choosing two colors on this circle that are not complementary, it will not be possible to obtain an achromatic mixture. In addition, all colors are not present on the color circle. These are called nonspectral colors and can only be obtained by mixing at least two colors. Purple is an example of nonspectral color.

The addition of color also obeys another law. If we mix equal amounts of different colors, the resulting brightness is greater than the average brightness of the colors used in the mixture. Also, if the mixed quantities are unequal, the resulting brightness is closest to that of the color presented in highest quantity.

Finally, note that there are other types of color mixtures. These other color mixtures are reported below in a section about color effects and illusions.

5.4   Theories of Color Vision

Two major views have long been opposed when attempting to explain color vision. A first view point, supported by Thomas Young in the early nineteenth century and also by Hermann von Helmholtz a few decades later, is known as trichromatic theory of Young-Helmholtz. Essentially, this theory states that color vision depends on the presence of three types of receptors in the eye. It is postulated that these receptors are sensitive to all wavelengths, with a maximal sensitivity for a given length. These receptor types are more sensitive to blue, green, and red. In fact, Young and Helmholtz knew that, for a person having no color vision deficit, an additive mixture of red and green gives yellow. So they explained the vision of yellow by the excitation of the receptors of red and receptors of green. Indeed, according to them, any color could be explained by different excitation levels of the three receptor types.

Later in the nineteenth century, various observations not compatible with the trichromatic theory led Ewald Hering to develop another theory of color vision. In particular, Hering observed that people asked to choose colors that do not seem to be a mixture tend to discern four, and not three, primary colors: blue, green, red, and yellow. He also observed that people never report perceiving a greenish red or a yellowish blue. Moreover, the fact that people perceiving neither red nor green can perceive yellow was also a major objection to the trichromatic theory of Young-Helmholtz. Finally, Hering also knew that prolonged exposure to a color can create a strange effect, as discussed below.

Thus, Hering rather proposed the *opponent process* theory to account for the wide range of perceived colors. This theory states that color perception is based on the operation of pairs of opponent colors. These pairs are red and green, blue and yellow, and white and black to reflect brightness perception. In this way, if a neuron is excited by the presence of a color, it will be inhibited by the presence of the opposite color.

Interestingly, contemporary data from physiology provide support for both theories. With a technique called microspectrophotometry, it is possible to quantify the proportion of light, for a given wavelength, absorbed by the photoreceptors. Thus, it was possible to observe that there are actually three types of cone, each having a maximum light absorption for different wavelengths, as suggested by the theory of Young and Helmholtz. The exact value of these wavelengths varies somewhat depending on the study. For instance, maximum absorptions were reported at 420, 530, and 560 nm in macaques (Bowmaker, Dartnell, & Mollon, 1980) and 425, 534, and 564 nm in humans (Bowmaker & Dartnell, 1980). Since these values loosely correspond to red, green, and blue, respectively, some authors use the terms the red cones, green cones, and blue cones (sometimes also called γ, α, and β fibers). Although it may be simpler to adopt these terms, especially in the context of the trichromatic theory, it is more accurate to call them S, M, and L to respectively designate the cones having maximum light absorption at short, medium, and long wavelengths. Indeed, as the values reported above indicate, the values are closer to the long wavelengths than to the short ones.

Other physiological data rather allow to support the other theory of color vision, that of Hering. However, contrary to the contention of Hering, these opponent processes are not located at the receptor level. An investigation of the functions of nerve cells beyond photoreceptors reveals that some cells actually work according to an opponent principle. This investigation was conducted at different levels between the photoreceptors and the striate cortex, particularly at the level of the ganglion cells and of the lateral geniculate nucleus. In both cases, the opponent responses are comparable. Based in particular on the wavelength at which a cell becomes inhibited rather than excited, DeValois, Abramovet, and Jacobs (1966) grouped the opponent cells of the lateral geniculate nucleus into four categories (see also DeValois & DeValois, 1988):

$$R + G - \quad R - G + \quad B + Y - \quad B - Y +$$

where R = red, G = green, B = blue, and Y = yellow and where + means that cells are excited by the presence of the designated color and − means that they are inhibited (Fig. 5.7). We also find two types of non-opponent cells in the lateral geniculate nucleus. These cells respond to all stimulations, either by increasing their activity (white+/black−) or by decreasing it (black+/white−).

Thus, color vision can be explained with a system that is somewhat of a compromise between the theories of Young-Helmholtz and Hering. Specifically, this system, shown schematically in Fig. 5.6, has two levels: the three types of cones transmit information to a more central level of processing (DeValois & DeValois, 1975). In the retina, the information is captured by three types of cones reacting optimally to their wavelength: C cones to short waves, M for medium waves, and L for long waves. At ganglion cell level, the information coming from the photoreceptors exert an activating or inhibiting effect on some of the four types of opponent cells or two types of non-opponent cells. For example, the cones sensitive to shorter wavelengths would activate the B+Y− system and inhibit the Y+B− system.

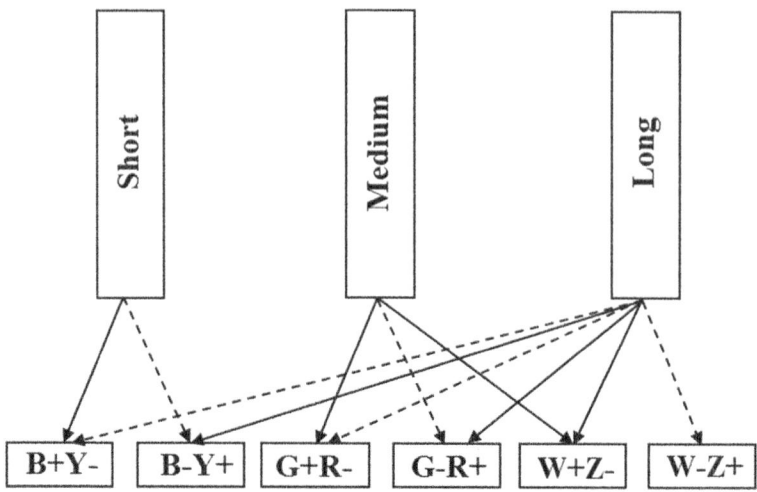

Fig. 5.6 Compromise theory by De Valois and De Valois where color vision depends on the neural activity at two levels. (1) Cones are particularly sensitive to short, medium, and long wavelengths. (2) At the next level, there are opponent (the *four rectangles* on the *left*) and non-opponent (the two on the *right*) processes. *B* blue, *Y* yellow, *G* green, *R* red, *Z* black, *W* white, + activation, − inhibition, *continuous line* activation, *dotted line* inhibition

With such a two-level system, it is possible to explain hue with the excitation of the R+G−, R−G+, B+Y− and B−Y+ opponent processes. These processes also help explain why complementary colors cannot coexist. For example, we cannot perceive greenish red, but perceiving greenish blue makes sense (if the S and M cones are excited). Brightness would be explained by the activity of non-opponent white-black and black-white cells. Finally, saturation would depend on the fact that the activity of the opponent processes would be higher than the one of the White + Black− system.

Finally, color perception probably also depends on other complex mechanisms. Researchers have identified, in the striate cortex, clusters of cells that react only to colors (Livingstone & Hubel, 1987; Michael, 1978). A property of these cells is to have double-opponent receptive fields.

5.5 Chromatic Effects

While there are only few definitive explanations of the different perceptual phenomena related to color, it remains relevant to describe some of them. Some phenomena reveal that color is not simply a matter of wavelengths or physical stimulation. It is possible to obtain one particular color mixture depending on how these colors are presented. It may indeed happen that the brain makes an average synthesis of what is presented. Colored portions of a visual field may be confused because of their density. For example, if small squares of two different colors alternate horizontally and vertically, you can distinguish them from each other if you are close to the image. You discern correctly the color of each square. However, if you sufficiently move away from the image, you will reach a point where you will no longer distinguish colors correctly. The entire image will appear in a different color, which will indeed be the synthesis of the two colors used. This phenomenon is referred to as a spatial optical mixing. In the same vein, it is possible to create conditions leading to a temporal optical mixing. This time, you might very well discriminate between two colors on a circle, but if you were turning the circle (as when spinning a top), this would lead, at a certain speed, to the inability to succinctly distinguish the two colors, and the brain would be forced to make an average synthesis of the two colors.

The effects caused by temporal constraints are not restricted to cases involving colors. Sometimes, black and white arrangements, such as the one in Fig. 5.7, can generate different colors. If one spins such black stripes on white background, colors appear. Since these colors vary from one person to the other, this phenomenon is called subjective colors. According to Henri Piéron, a French psychologist who worked in the first half of the twentieth century, the configuration and the rotational speed of the disk would influence selectively the receptors to red, green, and blue as the receivers do not all have the same response speed. Other authors argue instead that the explanation is not located in the retina itself. The stimulation would reach the brain directly and would produce a sequence of neural events that would be interpreted, because of its resemblance to the actual effect of colored stimuli, as a chromatic stimulus.

The *simultaneous contrast* is a subjective enhancement of color differences. In other words, the perceived hue depends on the context (Fig. 5.8), and this context can accentuate differences. This could be caused, according to Helmholtz, by an unconscious inference about brightness. We will return to this concept of unconscious inference, in the context of depth perception (Chap. 7). For Hering, the effect would rather be due to lateral inhibition (which will be discussed in the next chapter). Essentially, this means that when a region of the reception system is excited by

Fig. 5.7 Arrangement in *black* and *white*—Benham's top—which allows, when spinning quickly, to create an impression of color

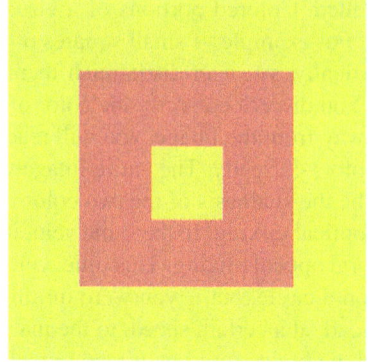

Fig. 5.8 Example of simultaneous contrast where the *pink square* in the *middle* appears *darker* on the *right* than on the *left*

Fig. 5.9 Is it possible to change this flag of Ivory Coast into that of France? Yes. You simply need to fixate on the flag above for a minute and then look at a *white surface*. After a few seconds, you should see new colors appearing

a chromatic stimulus, its neighboring regions remain insensitive to stimuli of the same color. What is obtained is rather the activation of the response to the complementary color.

In contrast to a simultaneous contrast, there are *assimilation or equalization effects*. This effect is a subjective attenuation of color differences or of brightness differences when stimuli are placed close to each other. In other words, this effect occurs when a color borrows somehow the color of its neighbor.

A fairly spectacular phenomenon occurs when fixating a surface, and then another surface, rather than looking at two stimuli spontaneously as was the case for simultaneous contrast or assimilation effect. This temporal phenomenon is called *afterimage*. When you fixate on a color image over a long period, say 1 min, then immediately after fixate on a white surface, you see an afterimage appearing. However, rather than seeing the initial colors, i.e., the ones you have previously been fixating, you will eventually see the complementary colors appearing on the white surface (Fig. 5.9).

According to some researchers, the prolonged exposure leading to the formation of consecutive images is due to the fatigue of receptors specialized in the perception of the presented color(s). If, after prolonged exposure, we look at a white surface, which contains all colors, there will be a greater response of the non-fatigued receptors. These receptors are indeed those responding to the complementary color(s). The existence of such a phenomenon in which the complementary colors appear after a fixation period provides support to the Hering's position described above.

Another form of color aftereffect, called the McCollough effect, is particularly fascinating (McCollough, 1965). The effect can be obtained by fixating each of the top gratings (see Fig. 5.10) for about fifteen seconds and then by looking at the other gratings below. The color of the perceived afterimage depends on the orientation of the bars (of the gratings). The color of the afterimages will tend to be red between the vertical bars but green between the horizontal bars. While it is believed that the

Fig. 5.10 Images required for producing the McCollough effect (see text)

consecutive images like the one described in the previous paragraph should be attributable to the neuronal adaptation at the retina level (a low level of processing), the McCollough effect would rather be caused at a higher processing level, i.e., where orientation is processed (namely, in the V1 area). And what would happen if you lean your head or if you turn the book at 90°? Try it!

Finally, just as there is a constancy phenomenon for other dimensions of visual perception, as we will see later, there is the so-called color constancy. With color constancy, it remains possible to recognize the true color of objects despite the chromatic variations of lighting, if these variations remain moderate. In other words, even if the daylight starts fading, or if an interior room is dimly lit (enough to stimulate the cones) or illuminated with light of a certain color (but not too intense), a red sweater should continue to appear red, as it is, for example, in the light of day. Thus, the visual system probably has the property of transmitting the differences in spectral composition, just like it can transmit intensity differences.

5.6   Clinical Aspects

There are several color vision disorders. The difficulty of discriminating yellow and blue affects equally men and women and touches less than 1 % of the population. The most common color vision problems are related to the discrimination of red and green and occur more frequently in men than in women (approximately 8 % against less than 1 %). This difference is caused by genes. Genes associated with these colors are located on X chromosome. Considering that women receive two X chromosomes instead of one as is the case with men, they will have this color vision disorder only if both X chromosomes are deficient. That is the reason why women are less likely to be affected by a red-green deficit.

There are three major categories of abnormal color vision. The first is called abnormal *trichromatism* and refers to a partial insensitivity to one of the three primary colors. In this category, we distinguish the protanomaly, deuteranomaly, and tritanomaly. People with protanomaly (approximately 1 % of men are affected) require a greater amount of red for perceiving as yellow the red-green mixture. With deuteranomaly, there is a need for a greater amount of green for perceiving as yellow a red-green mixture: it affects about 5 % of men. Finally, we refer to tritanomaly for describing the need for a greater amount of blue for perceiving as "blue green" a mixture of blue green.

A second major category of color vision deficit is called abnormal *dichromatism* and consists in a complete insensitivity to one of the three primary colors. Thus, a protanope, who is blind to red (affecting approximately 1 % of men), sees in yellow and blue, since red and bluish green are seen as gray. A deuteranope is blind to green (affecting about 1 % of men) and also sees in yellow and blue since the bluish red and green are seen as gray. Finally, a tritanope sees only red and green, but this deficit is very rare. Purple and yellow green are seen as gray.

The third major category is *monochromatism*. Extremely rare, this problem means that vision is summed up in shades of gray. It is caused by the lack of functioning cones, and, therefore, there is no surprise that this problem results in a decreased visual acuity.

It should also be noted that color vision disorders can be caused by damage to the V4 area of the visual cortex and not only by a problem related to the functioning of the cones. Finally, it is possible to detect color vision problems using the Ishihara test. This test consists of a series of color plates on which appear through a set of colored points, numbers, or shapes. People with color vision disorders have difficulty, for example, to correctly identify certain numbers when they are unable to perceive the colors used to illustrate the numbers.

Chapter 6
Form Perception

We could say that we live in a world where our retinas are constantly assaulted from everywhere. Thousands of potential stimuli in the immediate environment may reach our eyes at any moment. These various stimuli result from the interactions between the surface properties and those coming from light sources (intensities and wavelengths). Moreover, our environment is sometimes stable, sometimes not; sometimes, things are moving and sometimes, we are moving. Therefore, there is constantly an incredible variety of stimuli on the retina. Nevertheless, we extract from all this information something intelligible; moreover, this task is completed without effort. This remarkable efficiency is made possible by the functioning of some basic mechanisms described below.

6.1 Perception of Contours

We can extract a shape in the environment because it provides brightness variations. These variations are such that there are boundaries between objects. We know that there is somewhere a given object because we perceive delimitation, or an edge, between this object and its surroundings. We call this edge a contour. This contour could be considered the elementary unit of form perception.

To fully realize the importance of a contour, just think about what happens during a snowstorm. When there is too much blowing snow, it becomes no longer possible to see anything, even when you try to keep your eyes open, because the field is evenly lit (in German, this phenomenon is referred to as a *ganzfeld*—i.e., complete field). If you want to experience a ganzfeld without waiting for the next snowstorm, simply try the following activity. Take two white plastic spoons or even the two halves of a white ping-pong ball, and draw a small but clearly visible colored line on the inside of the spoons or half balls. Then, just make sure to completely cover the eyes with spoons or half balls so that no light can enter. Keep your eyes open while fixating the inside line and avoid any eye movements.

© Springer International Publishing Switzerland 2016
S. Grondin, *Psychology of Perception*, DOI 10.1007/978-3-319-31791-5_6

You need to maintain this fixation activity for several seconds so that the line remains at the same place on the retina.

What happens after a few seconds (less than a minute)? If there was no movement of your eyes, the line disappears. For perceiving form, even just a single line, it takes brightness variations between this form and its environment. We clearly see the line at first, but eventually lose sight if we prevent the visual system from restoring the perception of a contour. In fact, the image never remains stable for long on the retina. The image on the retina keeps moving because there are always small eye movements called microsaccades. These small involuntary eye movements create variations in time on the receptors of the retina. What the experiment with the spoons or half balls teaches us is not only that it takes contour perception to see but also that it is necessary, for avoiding the disappearance of the contour, that the image does not stabilize on the retina.

6.1.1 Edges and Subjective Contours

The contour depends mostly on the presence of an edge. The latter can be defined as a change in luminance or spectral composition occurring somewhere in the environment. Most often in the environment, contrast or texture changes will create edges. In other words, the contours are typically due to a physical phenomenon, namely, the presence of boundaries. In this case, we sometimes refer to it as the first-degree contours (or first-level contours).

As shown in Fig. 6.1, the presence of an edge is not always necessary for the formation of a contour. It is possible to perceive contours without any physical changes. Such conditions are referred to as subjective contours or second-level contours. We also refer to the term emerging contours to describe these cases where a contour is perceived although there is absolutely no physical variation producing it.

In short, perceiving a form requires to perceiving contours. The detection of these contours depends mostly on the presence of an edge caused by the heterogeneity in the stimulation. The perception of these edges also requires that variations of this stimulation occur on the retina. These variations are made possible by eye

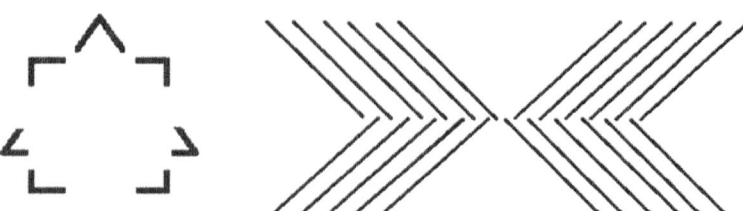

Fig. 6.1 Examples of subjective contours. You can observe a *triangle* and a *square* on the *left* and a *horizontal line* on the *right*

microsaccades. Finally, even in the absence of edges, there may be contours, called subjective, but their presence still requires the presence of special conditions in the environment as shown in Fig. 6.1.

6.1.2 Lateral Inhibition

There is a basic mechanism in the visual system for increasing brightness variations that generate a border. When light reaches the retina at a given point, what is located just next to this point undergoes inhibition. The mechanism by which the activity of certain nerve cells affects that of its neighbors is called *lateral inhibition*. This phenomenon, first reported by Keffer Hartline and Floyd H. Ratliff, is a fundamental notion of retinal physiology.

Hartline and Ratliff (1957) worked on the visual system of horseshoe crab. This animal has the distinction of having a series of small elementary eyes, called ommatidia, rather than a dense neural network. This feature makes it easier to stimulate each eye when the effect of lateral inhibition is demonstrated. Each ommatidium can somehow be compared to the ganglion cell of the human visual system.

In the work of Hartline and Ratliff, the electrical activity of a nerve fiber, say A, is collected by means of an electrode. When the receptor corresponding to fiber A receives light stimulation, the electrical activity increases, indicating that the activity is linked to the stimulation (Fig. 6.2). When only one receptor corresponding to a neighboring fiber, B, is stimulated, the electrical activity collected from fiber A is

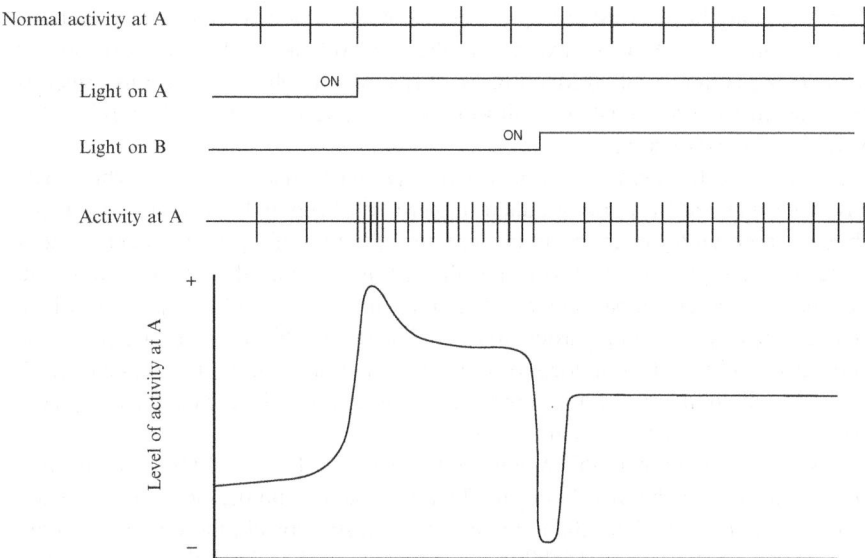

Fig. 6.2 Illustration of the lateral inhibition effect exerted on a cell, *A*, previously activated by a light source, by the arrival of a light stimulus to a cell, *B*, located close to *A*

not affected. This reflects the independence of the activity of B on A when there is no direct stimulation on A. In a case where light stimulation is maintained on A, and another light stimulation excites B, then the electrical activity observed earlier on fiber A is decreased. In other words, the activity on B exerts lateral inhibition, that is to say, it reduced the activity of neighboring fiber A.

The strength of this inhibition depends essentially on two factors: the proximity between the nerve cells involved and the strength of the stimulation on the inhibitory cell. The stronger the activity of the inhibiting cell, the greater the inhibition; similarly, the closer the inhibited and inhibitory cells, the greater the inhibition effect.

Mutual effects of nerve cells or fibers on each other can be quite complicated. Suffice to say, there may be a decreased inhibitory effect in a case like the following one: Given fibers A, B, and C arranged in this order. B has some inhibitory effect on A when fiber C is not stimulated. However, when light stimulates C, the activity on C inhibits the activity of B. By having a reduced activity, B exerts in turn a less pronounced inhibitory effect on A. Thus, the electrical activity of A is higher if the fibers A, B, and C are stimulated compared to when only fibers A and B are stimulated. The activity recorded from A in the condition in which A, B, and C are stimulated remains nevertheless below that normally observed when only fiber A is excited.

6.1.3 Mach Bands

There are many fascinating perceptual effects which can be explained on the basis of lateral inhibition. A classic example of the effect of lateral inhibition is illustrated by the demonstration called Mach bands. Ernst Mach, who revealed this effect, is the same Austrian physicist and philosopher who gave his name to the unit used to express the speed of sound.

Consider the following situation where, say, black (dark gray) and white (pale gray) are separated by a gray gradient (upper part of Fig. 6.3). Although black and white are both uniform (even luminance), the insertion of a gray gradient changes the perceived brightness: the black and white are not perceived anymore as uniform. Most people perceive a particularly small dark line (very black) on the side where the luminance is low and a particularly pale line (very white) on the side where the luminance is high. At these locations, on each side of the gray, thus appear Mach bands. The main interest of this demonstration is therefore located at the two places where luminance changes occur.

It is possible to explain this Mach band effect with the lateral inhibition exerted by nerve cells on each other. For example, if we take two points close to each other, near to the midpoint where the luminance is uniformly black, these two points are subjected to similar levels of inhibition caused by neighboring cells to the left and to the right. Thus, their brightness is the same. If we rather take a point X where the luminance change begins, then the inhibition exerted by the left and by the right

Fig. 6.3 On the *lower panel*, changes in luminance (*black line*) and brightness (*green line*) corresponding to the *black and white image* (*upper panel*). *Arrows* indicate Mach bands. It is a little darker under the *left arrow* and a little brighter under the *right arrow*

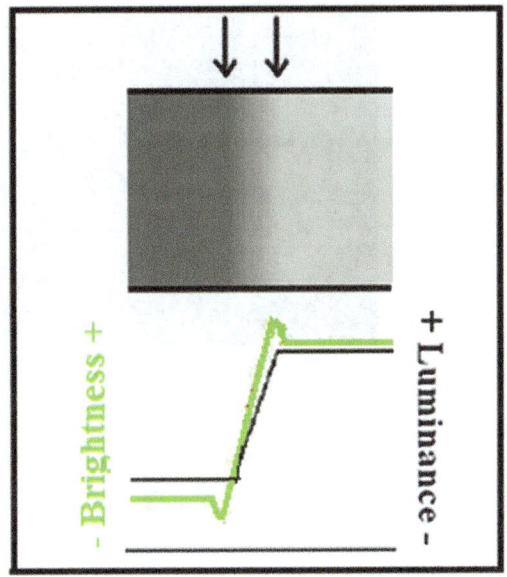

cells is not the same. If the transition initiates a luminance increase, the proportion of white of the physical stimulus increases, and, thus, the inhibition caused by the cells on this side on point X is larger than that exerted by the cells on the other side. So this transition line appears darker as it undergoes more inhibition. The same reasoning can be applied to the reverse situation: where a decrease in luminance begins as the inhibitory effect decreases. At this point of transition appears a brighter thin band.

One can also observe this Mach band phenomenon in Fig. 6.4 on which are illustrated a series of bands with uniform brightness. These bands do not appear uniform when viewed as a whole. If we do look at only one band, hiding somehow the others, then its brightness is uniform because the luminance of a given band is uniform. It is the activity exerted by the ones on the others that determines the level of neural activity of each cell and, consequently, the brightness. In brief, the figure shows a series of lateral inhibition effects.

6.1.4 Factors Influencing the Perception of Contours

Many factors may influence the creation of contours. For example, contours are perceived more easily when the visual acuity is greater. The acuteness being greater at the fovea, the contours appear more clearly in this region. The further away an image is moved from the fovea, the less clear the contours are. Similarly, subjective contours shown in Fig. 6.1 are examples of the influence of the spatial context on the creation of contours.

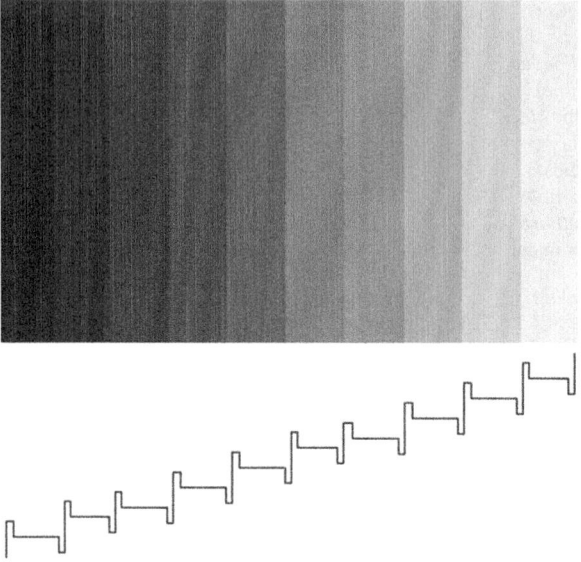

Fig. 6.4 Another illustration of the Mach bands where a series of stimuli, each of uniform luminance, appear *brighter* on the *left side* and *darker* on the *right side*

The formation of a contour takes a minimum of stimulation intensity. The intensity depends on the number of photons absorbed by the photoreceptors. Indeed, the
ability of these photons to produce an effect depends on how long the eye has been
stimulated. It takes a minimum of exposure time for a stimulus to be detected.
Photons can benefit from a temporal summation effect. If their arrival is not sufficiently close in time, they lose that benefit. This is essentially what Bloch's law
refers to. It can be summarized as follows:

$$I \times T = C$$

where the interaction between the intensity, I, and the exposure time, T, results in a
constant visual effect, C. If a stimulus is very intense, it can be detected even if
presented for a very short period, whereas a weaker stimulus will be detected only
if presented for a longer period.

In fact, the interaction between time and intensity applies only for very short
exposure times, i.e., of less than 100 ms. Beyond this period, the only crucial factor
is the fact that the intensity is sufficient or not for perceiving a stimulus. This 100-
ms value holds for rods; for cones, this value would rather be 50 ms. Note that there
is also a law, Ricco's law, which applies only to the fovea. According to this law, the
detectability of stimuli is a combination of the intensity and of the stimulated area.

There are different demonstrations which illustrate the importance of the exposure duration in the perception of contours. In this regard, an old experience of
Werner (1935) is most relevant. In this experiment, a black circle and a black ring
are presented alternately to a participant. The outer contour of the disk corresponds

Fig. 6.5 *Disk* and *ring* used in the experiment reported by Werner (1935). See text for explanation

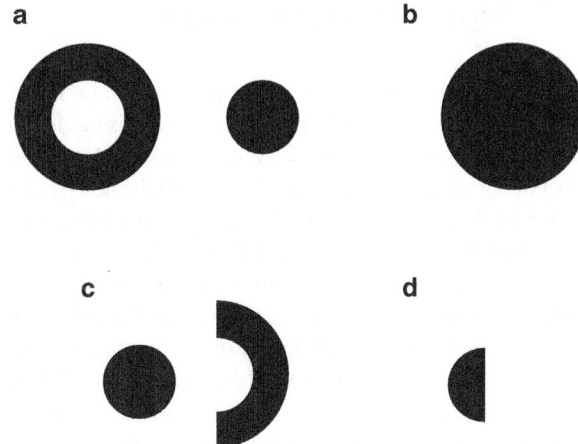

exactly to the inner contour of the ring (Fig. 6.5a). The experimenter varies the exposure time of stimuli and the pause time between exposures. When the time interval between stimuli is smaller than 100 ms, the participant perceives a full circle (Fig. 6.5b). If the interval between stimuli is more than 200 ms, the subject sees alternately the disk and the ring. Pauses with a duration ranging from 100 to 200 ms lead the participant to perceive only the ring. Thus, depending on a temporal factor, a masking effect may occur. The formation of the inner contour of the ring prevents the contour of the disk to be seen. And if it is the disk and only a half-ring (Fig. 6.5c) that are presented for 100–200 ms, only the half-disk can be detected (Fig. 6.5d).

6.2 Gestalt: Perceptual Organization

A century ago, Max Wertheimer developed a fine and influential way of approaching the study of form perception. The school of thought, known as Gestalt, which means form (or "whole form"), also received contributions from Wolfgang Kohler and Kurt Koffka, other German specialists of the psychology of sensation and perception, and collaborators of Wertheimer. The aim of the Gestalt psychology, which encompasses all the work on perceptual structuring, was to explain how the visual system combines the various elements available in the visual field.

There is in this notion of Gestalt the idea that perceiving is more than the summation of the sensations produced by stimuli. There is an organization of these stimuli. A person organizes the elements of a visual scene for extracting meaning. The organization of these elements includes two aspects that will be described in the following paragraphs. There is firstly the distinction between figure and ground and secondly the grouping of elements according to some characteristics sometimes called the laws of Gestalt.

6.2.1   Figure/Ground Distinction

When looking at a visual field, some parts are different from others. We look in a particular way in order to highlight some parts of this field. In a task as simple as looking at a piece of art on a wall, there is a way of looking. Our gaze is focused on the dominant object of our visual field, the piece of art, and the nearby field, the wall, serves as a background. So there is a fundamental distinction, the figure as opposed to the ground, in our way of looking. These two parts of the field have their own characteristics.

In a visual scene, the contour seems to belong to the figure rather than to the ground. The figure looks like something and appears to be closer than the ground. There may sometimes be an ambiguity in the figure, as shown in Fig. 6.6, which can be solved according to the way of looking. In Fig. 6.6, on the left, the black part is perceived as the ground, and, consequently, white diamonds are perceived spontaneously. In Fig. 6.6, on the right, white diamonds are much less likely to be perceived spontaneously. Indeed, it is much easier to imagine that the white part can be the ground in the right than in the left figure. Consequently, we perceive much more easily that there are black diamonds in the right figure.

In general, a figure has a shape and some meaning, whereas the background is rather disorganized. Indeed, several objective factors determine this figure/ground distinction. These factors are illustrated in Fig. 6.7. These factors are reported to be objective because they are determined by the stimuli. An image placed in a vertical horizontal orientation will be more readily perceived as a figure than if it is placed in diagonal directions. Thus, it should be easier to perceive a white cross in the left portion of Fig. 6.7a than it is in the right portion. In this latter case, due to *orientation*, we perceive more spontaneously the gray cross than the white cross. Similarly, a smaller (or thinner) image is more easily perceived as a figure than a larger image. This factor is called the *relative size*. Thus, in Fig. 6.7b, we perceived more easily a

Fig. 6.6 Illustration of the propensity to see, on the *left*, *white diamonds* on a *black background* and on the *right*, *black diamonds* on a *white background*

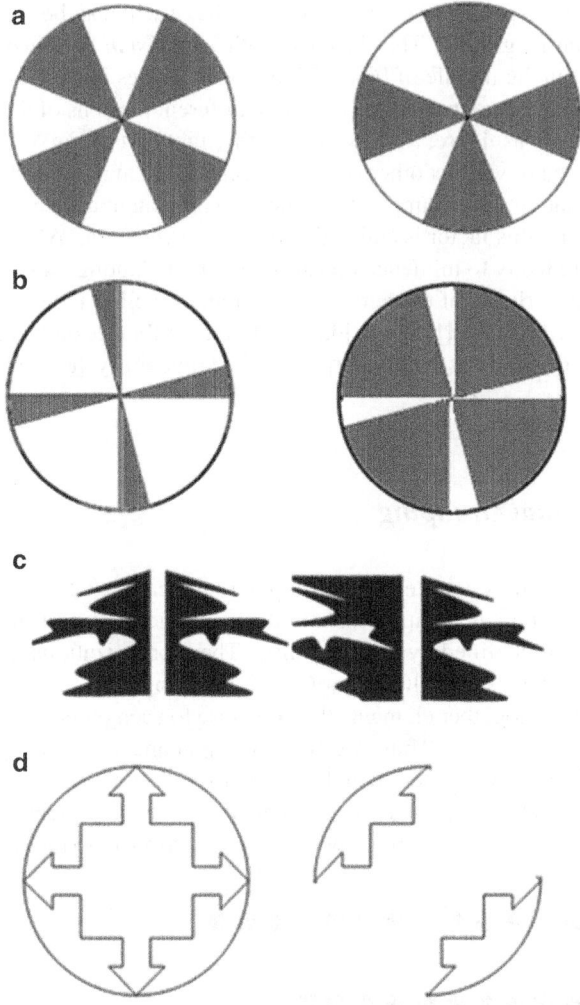

Fig. 6.7 Objective characteristics of the figure/ground segregation: (**a**) orientation, (**b**) size, (**c**) symmetry, and (**d**) inclusion (see text)

gray cross than a white cross on the left, but the reverse on the right. In fact, the thin crosses on Fig. 6.7b are more spontaneously perceived than the crosses on Fig. 6.7a.

Another very powerful factor is *symmetry* (or regularity). When objects or figures are symmetrical, they are more likely to be perceived as figures. Thus, because the four black pieces of Fig. 6.7c are on a white background, they tend to be perceived as figures. However, it would have been possible to perceive a white figure between the two black parts in the center, but being very irregular, this white figure cannot be spontaneously perceived. In addition, the two black parts on the left being symmetrical, they are easily perceived, more than are the two rightmost black portions of the figure.

When an image is inside another, chances are that it will also be recognized as a figure rather than as ground. This factor is called *inclusion* (or *surroundedness*). Thus, the square in the middle of Fig. 6.7d, on the left, does not act like ground but is part of a complex figure in a circle. That said, different portions of the circle could have been perceived as figure, as illustrated in the right part of Fig. 6.7d.

Note that there are various other objective factors that may contribute to figure/ground differentiation. For example, the patterns within an image can be crucial for perceiving a figure; this factor is called the *internal articulation*. Also, various subjective factors are likely to influence this differentiation. Among these factors, there is the previous experience of the person perceiving, as well as the elements toward which attention is directed. That individual traits exert influence on what is extracted from a given visual scene is hardly surprising for clinical psychologists using projective tests.

6.2.2   Perceptual Grouping

The visual perceptual system tends to group automatically, that is to say, without cognitive effort, certain elements present in the visual field. This grouping is based on basic principles identified by the Gestaltists. These organizational principles are sometimes referred to as Gestalt laws or Gestalt grouping rules.

We tend to group together elements that are close to each other. This tendency is called the law of *proximity*. Thus, we perceive spontaneously, in Fig. 6.8a, four groups of three elements rather than 12 elements. A series of elements may be equidistant from each other, but some of them can be grouped together because of their resemblance. This is what the law of *similarity* stipulates (Fig. 6.8b). A third

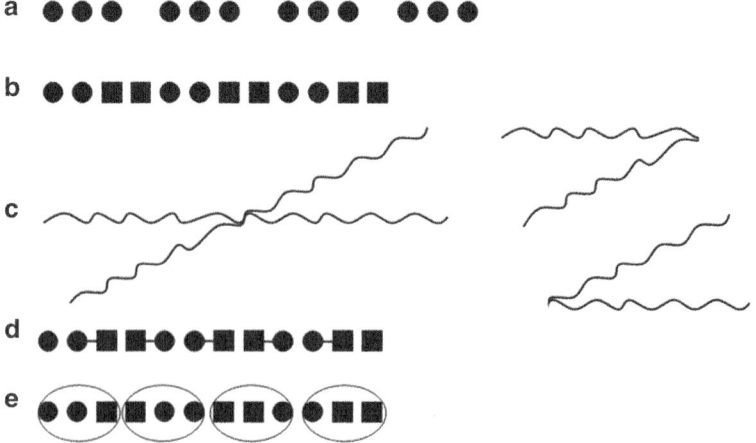

Fig. 6.8 Illustration of the Gestalt laws: (**a**) proximity, (**b**) similarity, (**c**) good continuation, (**d**) connectedness, (**e**) common region

law, known as the *good continuation*, reveals that the elements of a set forming a continuous series, or are part of the continuity relative to each other, tend to be seen as if they were one unit. Two intersecting lines are perceived in Fig. 6.8c, rather than the two items shown just to the right of these lines.

More recently, in what might be called a modern Gestalt, other perceptual organization principles were reported. These new principles are indeed very powerful. The first is called *connectedness* (or uniform connectedness). The fact of connecting elements together, as is shown in Fig. 6.8d, has more impact than the principles described earlier. Similarly, items that are part of the same region are seen as if they belong to the same entity. This principle, known as *common region*, is illustrated in Fig. 6.8e.

Furthermore, there are other laws of Gestalt, for example, the law of *closure*. According to this law, the visual system tends to see figures or objects as if they were complete, be it fully or in part; if the figure is not complete, the visual system manages to reach closure (see subjective contours, Fig. 6.1). Also, the more regular and symmetrical a shape is, the more it imposes itself to the perceptual system. This is known as the law of the *pragnanz*, also called the *law of good form* (and sometimes law of symmetry). Finally, another very powerful factor that organizes the visual perception is related to the fact that some elements might be in motion. If elements of a visual scene move in the same direction, they are perceived as being grouped together. This is called the law of *common fate* (or of *common motion*).

6.3 Theory of Multiple Spatial Channels

A very original way to address the issue of form perception was proposed in the late 1960s. This approach, developed by F. W. Campbell and J. G. Robson, is based on spatial frequency analysis and is sometimes referred to as the multiple spatial channels theory (Campbell & Robson, 1968).

6.3.1 Basic Concepts

The multiple spatial channels theory is based on a simple and clever idea: each image can be decomposed into a series of cyclical variations in luminance. The reader already familiar with the physical bases of auditory perception knows that sound can be interpreted as pressure variations over time. Similarly, a visual scene can be described as luminance variations, but instead of being described as variations as a function of time, they are described as a function of space.

A full understanding of this theory requires knowing that the size of the retinal image depends on the distance from which an object is viewed. For an image of a given size and for a given distance, the size on the retina is twice as small if the image is twice as far. When we look at an image, the spatial frequency thus depends on variations in luminance ("light/dark") and on the distance from which the image is perceived. For a given visual angle, there are a number of these variations. For example, an object with a diameter of 175 mm and located 10 m from the person subtends a visual angle of about 1°. A variation of periods alternating between light luminance and dark luminance is called a cycle. This makes it possible to express what is viewed on the following terms: the number of cycles per degree of visual angle. That is called *spatial frequency*, which is one of the four characteristics allowing the understanding of Campbell and Robson's idea.

A visual scene—a grating—like the one shown in Fig. 6.9 can be described by means of a sine wave. The *spatial frequency* is higher in C than in A or B. The difference between A and B is due to a second characteristic: the *contrast*. For a given cycle ranging from a light band to a dark band, the intensity variation is not the same. The light band is brighter in B than A. When the differences between light and dark bands are large, the contrast is high. If the contrast is too low for perceiving a difference between the two areas, it means that the contrast is below the visibility threshold. The contrast level can be quantified by means of a percentage scale ranging from 0 to 100 %, i.e., from the weakest (incapacity to perceive) contrast to the highest contrast.

Two more features complete the description of a visual scene. The gratings like those in Fig. 6.10 (left column) are identical, but their position is not the same. It is their *spatial phase* that distinguishes them. Finally, the bars of the gratings can be more or less inclined. Those on the left column and those on the right column differ on the basis of a fundamental characteristic called *orientation*.

In everyday life, visual scenes are rarely that simple or as clear-cut as described in Figs. 6.9 and 6.10. Figure 6.11e, for example, is more complex. However, it contains a series of simpler elements. Using a mathematical procedure known as Fourier analysis, it is possible to decompose a complex scene on the basis of simpler elements, in this case a series of sine waves. The gratings in Fig. 6.11a, b are used to form the grating illustrated in Fig. 6.11d. If we add the grating in Fig. 6.11c to the ones in Fig. 6.11a, b (or to the grating of Fig. 6.11d), we obtain the complex figure

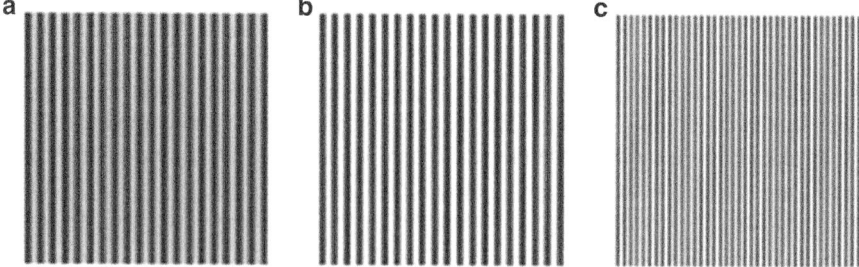

Fig. 6.9 Spatial frequency is much higher in (**c**) than in (**a**) or (**b**), but (**a**) and (**b**) differ because the contrast is higher in (**b**) than in (**a**)

Fig. 6.10 Gratings in the *left column* have different phases, whereas those in the *right column* have different orientations

Fig. 6.11 Grating (**e**) is complex, but is made in the end of the mixture of gratings (**a–c**); and grating (**d**) results from the mixture of gratings (**a, b**)

reported in Fig. 6.11e. Note that the spatial frequency in Fig. 6.11c is much higher than the one in Fig. 6.11b, which is itself much higher than that in Fig. 6.11a.

Although we do not consciously have the impression that they are there, each of the components of a grating like the one shown in Fig. 6.11e acts on the brain. These components excite different sets of neurons. For each component, there is therefore in the visual cortex a set of neurons that are specific to it. At the cortical level, for viewing a form, it is necessary to synchronize the activity of a series of specialized neurons.

In the context of Campbell and Robson's explanation based on spatial frequencies, such a set of neurons is called a channel. This channel essentially acts like a frequency detector. Each channel is sensitive to the spatial frequencies which extend over a narrowband. Also, because multiple channels are often activated at the same

Fig. 6.12 *Block image* of
Cosette, blurred when seen
from up close, but clearer
as we move away. Cosette
is a character from Victor
Hugo's *Les Misérables*,
drawn originally by
illustrator Émile Bayard

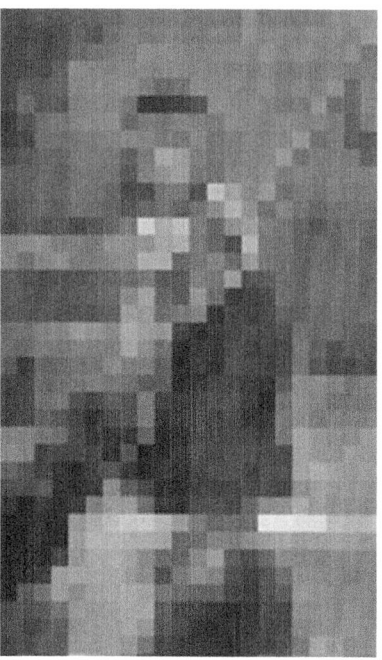

time, we talk about the theory of multiple channels, and more specifically about the multiple spatial channels theory, since it refers to spatial frequencies.

When using images made of squares like that reported in Fig. 6.12, it is possible to realize that perceiving a form means filtering what these images are in terms of the spatial frequencies that they contain. Depending on the distance between the observer and the image, it is not the same spatial frequencies that are involved, and, therefore, different specialized channels are activated. The squares add noise to the image. When we are at a normal reading distance, the image is not clear: a series of small squares are perceived. When we move away, the spatial frequency is changed and a clearer vision is restored.

On a more practical level, this means that if an image with squares is presented during the news on television to hide the face of a criminal or accused, you now know that you have better chances to identify the person if you move away from the TV! You also know that when you change the angle with which you are looking at something, you see things differently. This information will be precious the next time you visit a visual art gallery or museum where paintings are exhibits. Your impression on a piece of art might change if you adopt different perspectives. The effect is even more striking in a gallery like the Orsay Museum in Paris, for example, which exhibits the works of great Impressionist masters. Different angles and different distances allow to increase the appreciation of the works, for instance, of Van Gogh, Renoir, or Monet or of artists like Georges Seurat and Paul Signac who used pointillism to create impressions.

6.3.2   Contrast Sensitivity Function

The multiple spatial channels theory offers a new interpretation of the perception of form and, by the same occasion, a new way of approaching the study or the measurement of visual abilities. We are able to perceive images at different distances with the involvement of different spatial frequencies. However, for the different spatial frequencies, we do not have the same efficiency for perceiving. As is the case for the range of audible frequencies in the field of audition (Chap. 2), or visible wavelengths as we saw in the previous chapter, we are not sensitive to all spatial frequencies.

More specifically, just like it is possible to compensate some deficit in the perception of some auditory frequencies by increasing the loudness of the sound, it is possible to perceive an image, for certain spatial frequencies, only by increasing the contrast. In other words, the perception threshold has to be increased. This link between the spatial frequency and the perception threshold is described by what is called the *contrast sensibility function* (CSF). In brief, the contrast sensitivity is described as a function of the spatial frequency.

For humans, the sensitivity is at its maximum at about 3 cycles/degree. It is at this frequency that the threshold is the lowest. The extent of the sensitivity of the visual system varies from one animal species to another and depends on the light level. Given the demands of their environment, it is not surprising to learn that goldfish have a maximum sensitivity for images with a spatial frequency of about 0.3 cycle/degree, as opposed to the hawks that are crisscrossing the sky, searching for prey on the ground, who have a maximum sensitivity for spatial frequencies of about 30 cycles/degree.

This CSF concept has interesting practical implications. In fact, it measures the visual abilities more completely than does the traditional visual acuity test, the Snellen chart (Fig. 6.13). With the latter, the visual ability is only tested in an optimal condition, i.e., in a condition where contrast is high. Also, tests are executed

Fig. 6.13   A few lines from the Snellen chart

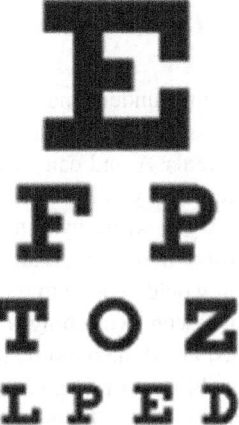

only with high frequencies. The visibility conditions we face in everyday life are not always optimal. For example, it may well happen that you have to drive a car in a more or less thick fog or when it is snowing or raining heavily. In such occasions, contrast is not at all at maximum. It may well be that people with the best visual acuity, as measured by the Snellen chart, do not have the greatest contrast sensitivity for low spatial frequencies. This issue also applies to aircraft pilots who must deal with all kinds of weather conditions, including flying through the clouds (Ginsburg, Evans, Sekuler, & Harp, 1982).

For historical purpose, note that the Snellen chart (or test) is a traditional eye examination tool for quantifying visual acuity. Developed by the Dutch Herman Snellen in the mid-nineteenth century, this tool is still used today. These charts are calibrated in different ways (different letter sizes). A conventional manner of using consists in reading from a distance of 20 ft (6 m in Europe). Letters have to be read with of a single eye, one letter at a time, down to the smallest letters that can be read. The goal is to determine whether a person can read at 20 ft what is normally read from that distance. When we say that a person has a 20/15 read, we say that that person reads at 20 ft what a person normally reads at 15 ft. This person has a good view.

6.4   Form Recognition

It is difficult to evoke form perception without mentioning the ability to recognize it. For recognizing a form, we have to have a representation of it. It therefore becomes necessary, for understanding the mechanisms of form perception, to refer to higher level concepts. This part of the chapter will not be just about what stimulates the retina but rather about what is kept from these stimuli and from the different visual scenes, objects, or faces.

6.4.1   Templates or Characteristics?

To fully understand the theoretical interest of the study of recognition, it is first necessary to understand the requirements of the task. All readers of this book know the letter A and can easily recognize it, whether it is a, **a**, *a*, A, **A**, or *A*. Yet, it is likely that you have never seen one or some of these As. Now imagine all versions of A you wrote by hand or even better and all versions of A that all humans have written in the past year. Even having seen only a very small percentage of these As, you would be able to recognize most of them. This indicates that we do not have to have seen everything a first time to make it possible to recognize some forms. Despite all the possible transformations of the same object, we do recognize it. This capability to recognize a visual stimulus in spite of the multiple changes it has undergone, or despite the new perspective for observing it, is called invariance.

A first model to account for this ability to recognize is called "template matching." According to this model, a template is kept in memory and superimposed on a form in order to verify to what extent this template and the form are similar. Once the learning of letter A is completed, it becomes possible to attempt to match the template that was learned with the one that is perceived. Such a theoretical perspective is based on the need to store a vast repertoire of images and templates. This idea has the advantage of being simple, but does not allow to really explaining invariance. We should learn everything a first time, which does not seem very economical when considering the space in memory such learning would require for storing information.

Rather than learning templates, perhaps we learn features. This perspective states that the stimuli are rather defined as combinations of basic features. If we take the previous example, learning letters, instead of making comparison with a template, it would rather be a comparison with the definition of what is retained. For letters, relevant questions would be, for example, the following: "Are there any lines with a vertical orientation? Are there any intersections? Are there any curves?" Given the specificity of certain cells for processing depending on the orientation (Chap. 4), this model has a certain plausibility from a physiological point of view (Hubel & Wiesel, 1968). Also, in an experiment in which the task is to determine whether the two letters presented are identical or not (Gibson, Schapiro, & Yonas, 1968, in Reed, 1982), the response time will be longer if the letters are alike (e.g., P and R), than if they are not (e.g., G and W). In other words, the processing time is longer and must be more complete if several features are in common.

So it seems that form recognition is based on features. But how does this process work? Does it work in sequence, where each element is processed successively, or is there some simultaneous processing, i.e., a parallel processing? According to Selfridge (1959), who developed a theory called the pandemonium, this processing is done in parallel and involves three steps. The different features (curve, angles, etc.) are first recorded, and then, specialized units (feature demons) take care of identifying them. Units representing letters (cognitive demons) then handle the need to reveal the level of agreement between the letter they represent and the recorded features. At a third level, units (decision demons) would be assigned to the identification of cognitive demons having demonstrated the highest level of agreement.

6.4.2 A Computational Approach

In the pandemonium theory, there is a first sign of a computational theory of form recognition. The goal within this approach is to develop programs (series of calculations) used to make connection between what occurs on the retina and the representation of objects and of the physical world. If neurophysiology provides information about the hard drive, it does not inform us about the dynamics (the processes involved) allowing to perceive and recognize form.

For Marr (1982), the perceptual representation is a construction involving different steps. There is a first filtering step which allows the extraction of the main features of an image. According to the filter properties that can be associated with receptor fields which have different sizes and allow to accentuating contours, it becomes possible to extract more or less rough idea of the image. For instance, narrower filters are more sensitive to higher spatial frequencies.

The information derived from this filtering operation thus results in a primitive sketch in two dimensions (2D). This is a fundamental first step in the computational theory of Marr. The different variations of light intensity reaching the retina are translated into features such as curves, intersections, etc. In short, the contours are detected and the main features of the image are drawn. This step can be compared to that of the draft in pencil performed by a painter. Next is a 2.5-D representation where the features are rather arranged according to the direction, depth, shadows, or texture. At this stage, the object is not yet a structured whole. All tridimensional information is not fully grasped. At this stage of processing, the sketch depends on the perspective of the observer, and, consequently, a change of perspective might prevent the recognition. The third stage is that of the 3-D model. It is centered on the object rather than on the observer's perspective. The surfaces are structured in volumetric components.

6.4.3 A Structural Model

Another model to account for the tremendous ability to recognize form was proposed by Biederman (1987). According to this author, this recognition is based on structural components. Somewhat along the line reported earlier for describing letters according to structural features, one could describe the objects based on a set of basic structures. One could compare this viewpoint to the idea that a few dozen phonemes allow to produce and recognize the thousands of words in a language (see Chap. 3). Thus, the description of all objects might be reduced to a series of basic components. Objects in memory would therefore be represented in the form of a spatial arrangement of geometric components. These components act in some way as phonemes in language. They are called geons, for "geometric ions." According to Biederman, there are 36 geons; Fig. 6.14 illustrates some of these. Note that these geons resemble cylinders that Marr and Nishihara (1978) were using to describe different forms.

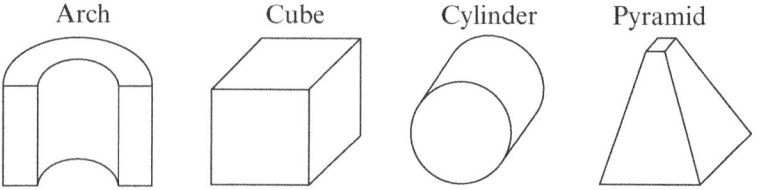

Fig. 6.14 A few examples of geons, the basic structures of the recognition-by-components model of Biederman (1987)

Geons can be extracted directly from 2D features. It is these geons and their relative position that determine the object. If we have a cylinder with a bow on the side, we have the representation of a cup; but if the bow is on top, it will be rather a bucket. Whatever an observer standpoint is, this description in terms of structures and their relationship does not change. With this model, it becomes possible to account for this crucial property, that is, spatial invariance. This model is interesting because it offers some resistance to constraints that sometimes accompany the perception of objects. For recognizing, the key point is to avoid the degradation of geons.

6.4.4   Agnosia

There exists a deficit specific to the identification or recognition of objects. This problem is called agnosia and is diagnosed as such when it is neither an intellectual disability nor a sensory disorder or a disorder of language. In general, it is said that agnosia is caused by perceptual problems or problems of representations in memory.

A first type of apperceptive agnosia may depend on the difficulty of extracting basic features like corners or edges. In other words, this is a very serious problem. This case is referred to as form agnosia. Another type could occur even when the features can be perceived, but in such cases, it is not possible to extract a whole configuration. This is called integrative agnosia. Another type of agnosia is called transformational. In this case, the agnosia is caused by the difficulty to recognize objects presented from a new angle.

Moreover, there are two categories of agnosia related to a problem of mnemonic representations. There is agnosia caused by the loss of structural representations, which entrains imaging trouble and the loss of a sense of familiarity with the object. The other kind of agnosia is the so-called associative agnosia, characterized by the inability to find the meaning of the object. This agnosia occurs because the semantic representation in memory is deteriorated or because it is not possible to access this representation.

Finally, prosopagnosia is the name given to disorder consisting of an inability to recognize faces, even one's own face. In such a case, the view of the face does not activate a sense of familiarity or biographical elements. In some cases, the affected person presented with a face is unable to identify whether the presented face is that of a young or of an old person, or that of a man or woman, or what facial emotion is expressed. Note in conclusion that face recognition is in itself a specific and fascinating subfield of study of form recognition (Tsao & Livingstone, 2008). One of the debated issues is related to the fact that the face would first be perceived as a whole (holistic model) as opposed to a viewpoint where the features and their spatial organization would be analyzed before face recognition.

Chapter 7
Depth Perception

The possibility to see the world in three dimensions remains quite fascinating considering the following peculiar fact: images arrive on the retina in two dimensions. Spontaneously, no one would doubt that there is a physical world that includes a third dimension. Nevertheless, the brain has to build this third dimension. The present chapter addresses this phenomenon, that of the construction of space or, more specifically, of depth.

In the preceding chapters, different aspects of visual perception sent the reader back to fundamental concepts of physics for understanding the nature of stimuli or to fundamental concepts of physiology or brain sciences for understanding biological bases of perception. In the present chapter, special attention is paid to psychological phenomena allowing to perceiving this third dimension. After a review of the main cues for perceiving depth, two phenomena are examined closely. The first one, perceptual constancy, is fundamental and is indeed not involved only in depth perception. The second one reveals cases, most often fascinating and fun, where these cues are misleading and induce illusions.

7.1 Cues for Perceiving a Third Dimension

The capacity of perceiving depth is based on the availability and contribution of several cues. These cues are kind of tricks allowing the brain to generate this impression of depth. However, using these tricks requires no voluntary effort; they are spontaneously activated by the data provided by the visual scene.

For understanding how these cues are studied in the field of perception, it is appropriate to make some distinctions between terms or concepts. First, for studying

© Springer International Publishing Switzerland 2016
S. Grondin, *Psychology of Perception*, DOI 10.1007/978-3-319-31791-5_7

the estimated distance, for example, researchers will distinguish absolute distance and relative distance. The idea of absolute distance, sometimes also called self-centered, refers to the estimation of the distance between an object and the one observing this object. In contrast, reference is made to relative distance, or exocentric distance, to designate the distance between the objects or between parts of these objects. If we generally find it hard to precisely estimate the absolute distance, we are rather good to decide if an object is closer to us than another object.

In addition to this absolute vs. relative distance distinction, it is important to keep in mind that the various depth cues that can be used can be classified in the following three dichotomous categories. Cues may be extraocular (nonvisual) rather than visual. Thus, information on depth might not be extracted specifically from the visual system per se, but from a source belonging to another sensory modality, namely, the kinesthetic system. Another useful distinction is the one between pictorial cues, which are static, and kinematic cues, which are dynamic, i.e., related to movement. Finally, there are binocular cues, as opposed to monocular cues. The presentation of the various cues below is based on this distinction.

7.1.1   Binocular Cues

The simple fact of having two eyes, and to have some distance between them, provides a better perspective on what is happening in our environment. It is possible to perceive depth with only one eye, but some cues require the joint operation of both eyes. These *binocular* cues are very powerful because they add precision to our appreciation of the third dimension.

7.1.1.1   Binocular Convergence

A first cue involving the contribution of both eyes is called *binocular convergence*. Looking at an object usually means that both eyes converge on it. If an object is far away, the angle between the focal point (the object) and the eye is small. If the object is close, the convergence angle is larger. According to the angle of convergence, the eyeballs are more or less displaced. These movements generate nonvisual cues. These cues are based on the kinesthetic information provided by receptors located within the extraocular muscles, i.e., the muscles that allow the movement of the eyes.

It is the convergence movement, rather than the state of convergence, which would provide the kinesthetic cues. This binocular convergence provides information on the absolute distance. Also, this source of information would be more effective when objects are close to the observer (say less than 6 m). Indeed, you can feel that there is some work being done in the eyeballs when you approach a finger to your nose and try to follow it with your eyes.

7.1.1.2 Retinal Disparity

A second binocular cue is called *retinal disparity*. The fact that there is some distance between the eyes is not trivial at all. This means that when looking at an object, an observer gets two points of view on it; in other words, for a given object, two images are formed. Disparity is the term designating the fact of receiving two images of the same thing, and binocular disparity refers to the disparity caused by the fact of having two eyes. Perceiving depth on the basis of binocular cues is also called stereoscopy (and sometimes binocular parallax), and the device designed to simulate a sense of depth with two different images of the same object, one for each eye, is called stereoscope.

It is easy to realize that each eye offers a unique point of view with the following exercise. First, place a finger 15 cm in front of you at eye level. By closing one eye and then the other alternately, you realize that different views of the finger appear. Equally important is the following fact. Place a second finger 15 cm behind the first, in the same axis. Now focus on the nearest finger, but pay attention to the farthest finger: it is seen in double. If you now focus on the farthest finger, but pay attention to the other one, it is now the closest one that is seen in double.

This difference in the clarity of the image as a function of the focus point is very important. It teaches us that not everything that is in our visual field is seen clearly. Horopter is the name given to the horizon line in front of us where vision is simple (no image seen in double); this line is actually an area called the Panum area. Depending on the distance of the fixation point, the size and shape of the area change slightly. Outside this area, the vision is in double. If simple vision is possible even if we have two eyes, therefore two images for one given fixation point, it is because for each given location on the retina of an eye, there is a precise correspondence point on the retina of the other eye.

Furthermore, it is important to note that the double vision of the close finger and that of the distant finger differ fundamentally. By placing two fingers as was done earlier and on focusing on the close finger, the farther finger is seen in double. By closing the right eye while continuing to focus on the close finger, the farther finger is seen with the left eye to the left of the close finger; now, by closing the left eye instead of the right one, the farther finger is seen with the right eye to the right of the near finger. Thus, when both eyes are open and we are fixating on a given point, what is located behind this point is seen in *uncrossed disparity*.

The demonstration works in the opposite direction. Now, the fixation point is the farther finger, but attention has to be allocated to the closer finger. By closing one eye and then the other alternately while keeping the fixation on the farther finger, one realizes that the closer finger is seen with the left eye to the right of the farther finger and with the right eye to the left of the farther finger. This is a case of *cross disparity*. The brain therefore benefits from a depth perception cue allowing to deciding whether object is in front a focal point or behind.

Finally, it should be noted that the visual field seen ahead binocularly covers a range of 120°. Added to this are approximately 40° of monocular vision to the left with the left eye and 40° of monocular vision to the right with the right eye.

7.1.2   Monocular Cues

Monocular cues of depth perception are sources of information about distance that remain available even when an observer uses only one eye. There are several monocular cues. Most of them are related to vision but one, *accommodation*, has a kinesthetic origin. In this case, the fact that an object is more or less distant causes a change in the shape of the lens. For instance, if an object is far away, the lens is less curved. Changing the shape of the lens requires changes in the contraction of the muscles involved in the accommodation process, and these muscular changes produce kinesthetic cues that the brain can interpret for assessing distance.

Because many objects have a typical size, it may happen that distance be estimated on the basis of this knowledge. For example, we know quite well the normal size of a card. If we are not under specific conditions such as those that cause optical-geometric illusions (see below), we can rely on the combination of this knowledge and retinal size for estimating distance. We call this index the *familiar size*. Thus, if we look at a coin that looks like a 25-cent coin, and if we do it in an environment where other depth perception cues are not available, we will assume that the size of this coin is normal for estimating how far away it is. If it should happen that this coin is actually smaller (because a friend is playing a trick or a researcher in psychology of perception studies the mechanisms of depth perception), this would be misleading, and the estimated distance would likely be incorrect.

Linear perspective is one of the most powerful depth perception cues, a cue that is most useful in the field of visual arts. When two lines like those shown in Fig. 7.1 converge to a vanishing point, they give a sense of depth. The points that are closer to each other appear to be farther away from the observer. The farther away is a part of the image, the smaller is the distance between each line on the retina. What we see in the real world in three dimensions can therefore be implemented on a two-dimensional image by adjusting the distance between the drawn objects and their size.

In fact, this linear perspective effect caused by the convergence could be considered a special case of a more general cue that James Jerome Gibson called *texture*. This is a mixture of both the linear perspective and the relative size of objects composing a visual scene. Most often we talk about texture gradients to denote the fact that the density and the size of the elements of a visual scene vary with their distance. Thus, as can be seen in Fig. 7.2, when dots are smaller and close to each other, they appear to be farther away. If what is viewed is farther away, the elements of the scene will be more compact.

Another visual cue for perceiving depth is called *occlusion*. This cue, also called *interposition*, refers to the fact that objects or parts of a visual scene are often hidden by other objects. What is covered necessarily appears to be farther away than what is causing occlusion. This powerful cue says nothing about the distance between the observer and the object, but gives an idea of the relative distance between objects. Figure 7.3 illustrates how powerful this cue is.

Fig. 7.1 Although the
rails are parallel, the
distance between them
appears to decrease from
the *bottom* of the image to
the *middle*, which induces
an impression of depth.
This is an example of
linear perspective

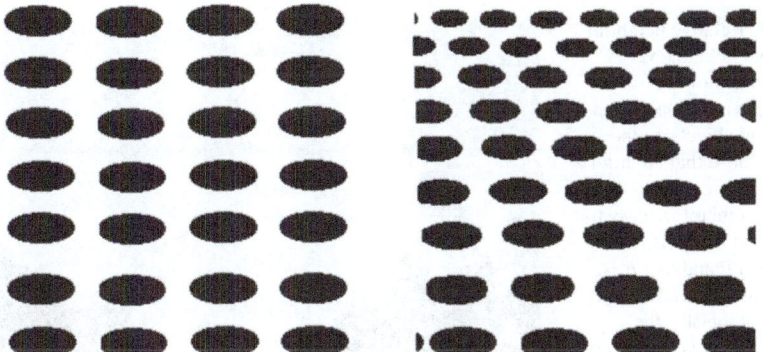

Fig. 7.2 When texture gradients are uniform, as on the *left*, no impression of depth is created; however, compressing points and using heterogeneous point size, on the *right*, give an impression of depth

Another cue based on the relationship between two objects allows to draw conclusions about their relative distance. This cue is called the *relative height*. The nearer an object is from the horizon point, the farther away it seems. Consequently, for the ground-related objects, i.e., below the horizon line (which is usually where our gaze is directed), the higher in the visual field an object is, the farther away it seems (Fig. 7.4). Conversely, for objects located above the horizon line, the lowest objects appear more distant.

Different arrangements of light and brightness can contribute to give an impression that objects or parts of the visual field are more or less close to an observer. For example, in the dark, the brighter of two objects is perceived as being closer.

Fig. 7.3 If we are presented only the two cards on the *left*, it is easy to figure out that the cards have the same size, with the five of hearts being farther away than the three of clubs. It is not possible to reach the same conclusion for the cards on the *right* due to the interference caused by the occlusion factor. Because the five of hearts covers part of the three of clubs, the five of hearts must necessarily be in front of the other card (i.e., closer); as a result, it is not possible to believe that these cards are the same size

Fig. 7.4 Relative height in the visual field is a very strong indicator for distance perception. When looking at objects on the ground, those that are high in the field are farther away. It is therefore easy to understand that *C* is farther away than *B* and that *B* is farther away than *A*. When looking at the sky, the relative height is still a cue, but now, objects that are low in the visual field are farther away. Thus, cloud *D* is more distant than cloud *E*, which is itself farther away than cloud *F*

This cue is called *relative brightness*. Somewhat in the same vein, the use of shading allows to create an impression that something is more or less distant. In the case of Fig. 7.5, it seems that some circles are concave and others convex. Interestingly, this impression can be reversed by rotating the book 180°. In fact, the angle of illumination from a light source might well change the perception of an object, of an image, or of a face.

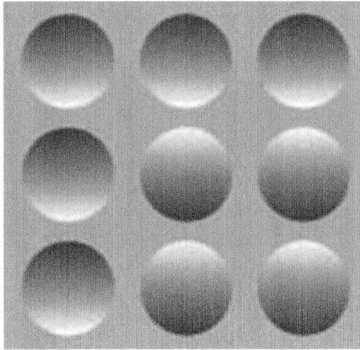 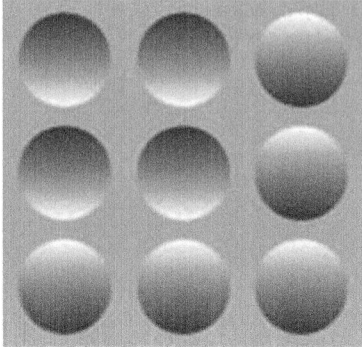

Fig. 7.5 Impressions of depth (concave versus convex) caused by shading. Images on the *left* and on the *right* are identical, but have been rotated 180°

It is also known that distance creates an attenuation of contours. This cue is called *aerial perspective* (or relative sharpness) and is more useful for estimating the distance of objects that are far away. The clearer the contour of an object, the closer the object appears because brightness contrasts are attenuated by distance. Thus, a car or even a mountain will appear much closer in clear weather than in fog conditions.

Another monocular cue, but linked to movement, is called *motion parallax*. The term parallax means shifting from one position to another. Here, we are talking about cases where a change is caused by the movement of an observer. To understand the relationship between the movement and the sense of distance, simply place a finger in front of you, and have your gaze fixated on it while moving your head to the left and to the right. When the head goes left, it seems that the finger goes right; when the head goes right, it seems that the finger goes to left. The wall behind the finger seems to go in the same direction as the head, but what lies between you and the finger (the fixation point) goes in the opposite direction. This provides an indication as to whether an object is in front or behind a fixation point. Even more important is the following point: the closer an object is, the greater the distance covered on the retina. Thus, the objects in the visual field give the impression of not moving at the same speed. The greater the speed, the closer the objects are. One can verify this statement by traveling on a road in the passenger seat: the gravel on the side of the road seems to fall quickly backward, whereas the mountain at some distance away, or a cloud, seems to follow you slowly. Now you know why it looks as if the moon follows us when traveling by car at night!

This section can be summarized by reference to Table 7.1 in which the cues for depth perception are classified as binocular or monocular, visual or nonvisual, and static or dynamic and on whether they are used to assess a relative or absolute distance.

In closing this portion of the chapter, it should be noted that the presence of certain cues in a visual scene determines the way we see. However, it may happen that

Table 7.1 Depth perception: summary and classification of cues

Cues	Type	Distance
Binocular		
Convergence[a]	K	A
Disparity	V	R
Monocular		
Accommodation	K	A
Familiar size	V	A
Relative height	V	R
Shading	V	R
Occlusion	V	R
Motion parallax[a]	V	R
Linear perspective	V	R
Texture	V	R

[a]Dynamic cues (other cues are static)
K kinesthetic, *V* visual, *A* absolute, *R* relative

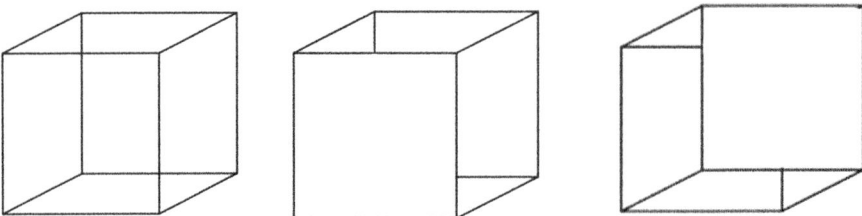

Fig. 7.6 Necker cube, on the *left*, could be perceived like the one at *center* or like the one on the *right*

the scene can be interpreted in different ways; in other words, cues may lead to some reversible images as is the case of the Necker cube (Fig. 7.6). On this figure, depending on what surface is perceived as occluding the other, a surface will be considered as being in the foreground or in the background. Similarly, the use in painting of some occluding effects can lead to the construction of pretty scenes that seem real, but could in no way be observed in nature. The Dutch artist Maurits Cornelis Escher has mastered the development of scenes involving this kind of deception. You may find some of the works of the artist if you just type his name on an Internet search engine. Similarly, typing "trompe-l'œil" on the Internet provides access to many other illustrations allowing to see how fine use of depth cues by painters can create powerful impressions, sometimes vertiginous, of a third dimension. We will return later to some particular impressions, namely, illusions, caused by the particular use of depth cues.

7.2 Perceptual Constancy

This section, which deals with the notion of perceptual constancy, could have been introduced at various places in this book, because it applies not only to size constancy but also to other dimensions, which will be detailed in the following paragraphs. The perceptual constancy is a basic mechanism of the perceptual system by which almost everything seems in order. Without that mechanism, we could not recognize anything. All physical stimuli would be chaos, and there would be no basis for perceiving.

What reaches the retina is continuously changing. If a chair is presented to an observer from an angle under which it has never been seen, the observer still manages to identify it as a chair. We can turn the chair in every sense and vary constantly the patterns of light energy it sends to the retina of the observer. This chair always maintains its objective characteristics, and the observer is able to know, without a shadow of a doubt, that two completely different energy patterns reaching his retina originate from the same object. In other words, seeing is not just a simple stimulation of retinal cells.

7.2.1 Types of Constancy

Among the different types of perceptual constancy, there is *shape constancy*. This constancy explains why an object maintains its shape even if different inclinations in different spatial planes cause as many variations of the projective image (see the previous chapter on form recognition). Similarly, under the *color constancy*, it is possible for an observer to recognize the hue of an object in spite of the fact that the light projected on this object changes its spectral composition, provided however that this change is not exaggerated. Also, the brightness of the object does not vary in spite of the differences in light intensity, and that is due to *brightness constancy*. Similarly, despite the differences in speed of the retinal image that can be caused by the distance in depth, it is possible to properly assess the speed of a moving object through a phenomenon referred to as *speed constancy*.

In the context of space perception, i.e., 3-D, the issue of perceptual constancy is closely linked to *size constancy*. The constancy refers to the capacity of maintaining the apparent size of objects or of people although the image size on the retina decreases with an increase of the distance between these objects or people and the observer. In other words, it is not because the retinal image of a person going away from the observer shrinks that this person appears to shrink. Unless there is in the environment a set of cues that may induce the observer in error, this observer continues to believe that this person is the same size.

7.2.2   Interpretations and Investigations

A classic question arises about the nature of size constancy: should distance be taken into account? In general, this question refers to the *size-distance invariance principle* (Kilpatrick & Ittelson, 1953). This hypothesis of invariance between size and distance basically states that an observer determines the apparent size on the basis of two combined elements of information, the perceived distance and the size of the retinal image. This idea is expressed by several authors in different forms. Thus, Helmholtz had already invoked the participation of a mechanism, the *unconscious inference*, to refer to the fact that the distance is taken into account in estimating the size of an object, this way of taking into account being settled without the help of conscious mechanisms. This theoretical perspective is also sometimes referred to as the algorithm theory (Epstein, 1977), as opposed to a relational theory. In the latter, the estimation of the size of an object or of person does not depend on some calculation of the distance between the observer and the object or person but rather on the relationship between the information available around the object or person. It is actually more a size-size type of relationship than a size-distance type. We will briefly return to this point of view in the next subsection.

The hypothesis about the need of taking the distance or not into account when size is evaluated has been tested in several empirical investigations. One way to illustrate the potential importance of distance in the evaluation of size is to use an afterimage. As we saw in Chap. 5 on color perception, a consecutive image is an image that remains somehow imprinted on the retina for a few seconds after prolonged stimulation. Remaining fixed on the retina, the image always maintains the same retinal size. The apparent size of this image depends on the distance of surface on which the image is projected. The farther away from the observer the projection surface is, the larger the image appears. This relationship between the apparent size of an afterimage and the distance from the observer to the projection surface is known as *Emmert's law*. This law illustrates the fact that the apparent size of an object depends not only on the size of the retinal image but also on the distance from which the object is perceived; therefore, apparent size likely depends on the fact of taking distance into account.

Among the various studies designed to test the size-distance invariance hypothesis, or the algorithm theory, the most classic is probably that of Holway and Boring (1941). In this experiment, some observers, including the authors, indicated the experimenter to adjust a comparison stimulus located about 10 ft (about 3 m) away. This adjustment was made for matching the size of a standard stimulus located in a long corridor at different distances, 10–120 ft (3–36 m), from the observer (Fig. 7.7). The stimuli, standard and comparison, were projected on screens. The images were uniform circular illuminations. In each experimental distance, the standard stimulus was adjusted so that the retinal image was kept constant, i.e., constantly subtended a visual angle of $1°$.

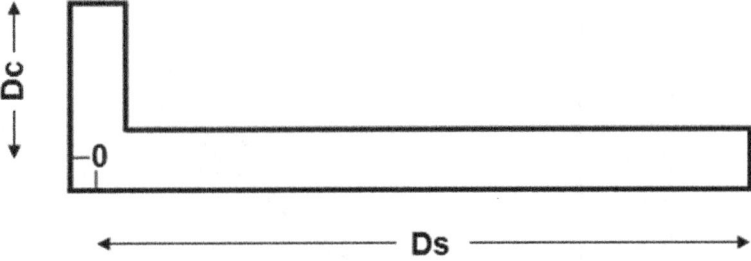

Fig. 7.7 Illustration of the experimental setting designed by Holway and Boring (1941). *Dc* distance of the comparison stimulus (10 ft ~ 3 m), *Ds* distance of standard stimulus (from 10 to 120 ft ~ de 3–36 m), *0* observer

The idea behind the experiment was to see if the adjustment of the comparison stimulus would be consistent with the actual size of the standard stimulus, as predicted by the size-distance invariance hypothesis. Thus, if the distance is not taken into account in the adjustment, the adjustment will always remain the same; however, if distance is taken into consideration, the adjustment will change as a function of the actual size of the stimulus or will get close to real size.

Holway and Boring pushed their reasoning a little further. If the distance is really considered, then different conditions for estimating distance should have an effect on the precision of the adjustment of the comparison stimulus. Thus, four experimental conditions were designed:

1. A binocular vision condition where the adjustment was expected to be the best
2. A condition where the only restriction was to use monocular vision
3. A monocular condition with vision through an artificial pupil, which was expected to reduce the cues provided by the motion parallax
4. A monocular vision condition through an artificial pupil and with low light conditions in order to reduce as much as possible potential sources of information on distance

Holway and Boring (1941) found that in conditions where cues were available for assessing distance, the adjustment of the comparison stimulus approximates the actual size of the object. In other words, even if the retinal size of the standard stimulus remains the same, the perceived size of the circular illumination changes according to the distance: the greater the distance, the greater the luminous circle, and the adjustment of the comparison stimulus is made accordingly. Figure 7.8 illustrates the results obtained in each condition. It should be noted that the loss of cues leads directly, as suggested by the slope of each function, to a decrease in the estimated size of the standard stimulus. All these results can be interpreted as supporting the size-distance invariance hypothesis, an idea often reported for explaining size constancy.

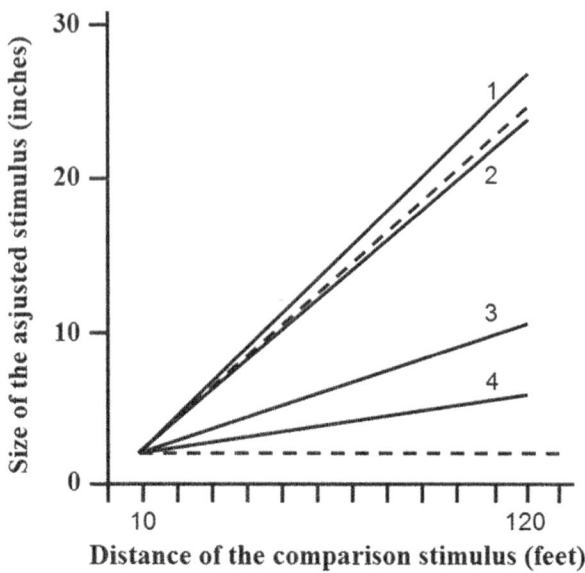

Fig. 7.8 Results of the experiment by Holway and Boring (1941—see their figure 22) where are grouped four experimental conditions: (*1*) binocular vision, (*2*) monocular vision, (*3*) monocular vision with artificial pupil, and (*4*) monocular vision with artificial pupil and reduced cues. The *broken lines* show the expected results would the perceptual constancy been perfect (*diagonal line*) and null (*horizontal line*) (1 in. ~ 2,54 cm; 1 ft ~ 30 cm)

7.2.3 Gibson's Perspective

Despite the elegance of this demonstration by Holway and Boring, other authors argue that this explanation based on the size-distance invariance can be faulted (Kilpatrick & Ittelson, 1953); it applies to the results in certain circumstances but cannot be a generalized. In fact, by removing cues of depth perception, the quality of the relational information is also reduced.

There is a radical position in the field of visual perception stating that there is no need for cognitive processing or inference mechanisms for estimating, for instance, depth. According to Gibson (1966, 1979), all the perceptual system needs is already available in the environment. In this Gibsonian perspective, everything that is in the environment (surfaces or objects) reaches the observer with specific physical characteristics. The movements of the observer determine what reaches the eye, and the material getting to this point is already organized. In the experiment by Holway and Boring, it was not possible for the observer to benefit from the cues normally provided by movements, especially in the condition involving to looking through an artificial pupil. Such an experimental design hinders the proper functioning, if not to say connivance, between the viewer and the environment.

Gibson therefore adopts what is referred to as an *ecological position* in which only natural situations can really contribute to our understanding of the visual system. In this Gibsonian psychology, the environment provides us spontaneously not only precise physical stimuli but also information relative to the function of what is observed (e.g., when it is an object). In other words, seeing a chair also activates in the brain of the observer what a chair is for, i.e., sitting down. In the Gibsonian terminology, the idea that perceiving is inseparable from the function is called *affordance* (that is to say, what is made possible by what is observed).

7.3 Illusions

The perceptual systems are generally very reliable and allow to be adapted to the requirements of the environment and its characteristics. Despite the effectiveness of these systems, it happens that an observer is misled when these characteristics are somewhat special. In the field of visual perception, such misinterpretations have quite amazing, and sometimes even spectacular, consequences. These misinterpretations are caused not by a system failure as the inability to maintain perceptual constancy but by the objective characteristics of the environment.

These errors are called optical illusions or optical-geometric illusions. As they depend on the normal functioning of the visual system, these illusions provide an opportunity to inform us about the nature of perceptual processes. They should not be confused with *hallucinations*, which are a phenomenon where there is an impression of perception even though there is no perceptual object around (no physical stimuli) or *mirages*, which are a physical phenomenon caused by reflections of light rays in particular conditions.

7.3.1 Variety of Illusions

There are of course very strong visual effects like those caused by the subjective contours described in the previous chapter. In addition to these effects, there are hundreds of illusions that an interested reader can discover by consulting older books (see Coren & Girgus, 1978 or Shepard, 1990) or some specialized websites on the Internet. We present here only some of the most classic or of the most spectacular illusions. Many of these illusions were discovered in the nineteenth century, and in most cases, a given illusion was named after the person who reported it.

The classification of these illusions into a limited number of categories remains a difficult exercise (Coren, Girgus, Ehrlichman, & Hakstian, 1976). Some classifications like that reported by Gregory (1997) require many distinctions; that of Piaget is simpler. Piaget is famous for his work on the development of intelligence, but nevertheless studied in depth the impact of perception on knowledge. Some of his works, including those grouped in a book entitled *Les mécanismes perceptifs* (Piaget, 1961), concern the illusions in particular and their changes in magnitude with age. Inspired by Alfred Binet, who is distinguishing innate vs. acquired

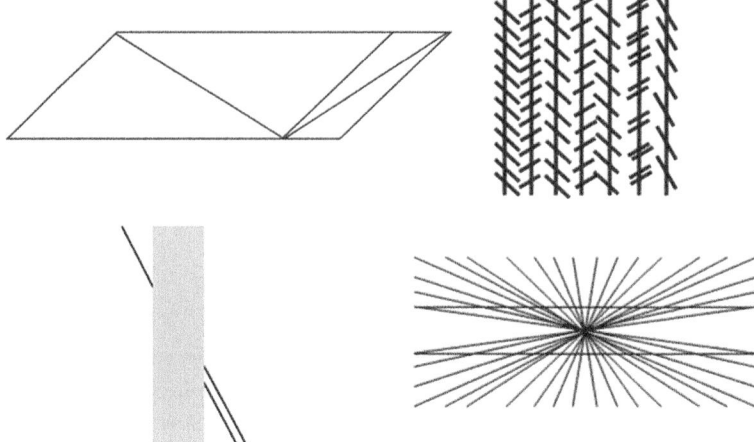

Fig. 7.9 In Sander's illusion (*top left*), the *diagonal lines* crossing the parallelograms are of the same length; in Poggendorff's illusion (*bottom left*), we are under the impression that, of the two segments on the *right of the gray rectangle*, it is the one on top that is in continuity with the one on the *left of the rectangle* (the reader should check); in Zollner's illusion (*top right*), the *vertical lines* are really parallel; and, similarly, in Hering's illusion (*bottom right*), the *horizontal lines* are really parallel

optical-geometric illusions, Piaget rather speaks in terms of primary illusions vs. secondary illusions. The fundamental property of a primary illusion, also called field effect, is that it does not vary qualitatively with age. However, their quantitative aspect, that is to say the strength of such an illusion, does vary with age. Also, Piaget does not say like Binet that the effect is innate. Secondary illusions are rather those arising from perceptual activities. These activities cause a decrease in some primary illusions and the emergence of new illusions.

Figure 7.9 reports a series of illusions based on angle effects. This category of illusions is very powerful. Among them, you will discover the spectacular Sander's illusion where the diagonal lines passing across parallelograms are surprisingly of the same length. Zollner's, Hering's, and Poggendorff's illusions are also based on angle effects.

Another example of angle effect, perhaps the best known, is the Müller-Lyer illusion (Fig. 7.10). This illusion could be explained by an assimilation effect or central tendency effect. According to this view, the EF and GH segments are taken into account in the estimation of segment AB (Fig. 7.10, right). Segments EF and GH being on average shorter than segments IJ and KL, it follows that the segment AB is perceived as being shorter than the segment CD.

For explaining the tendency to consider the segment AB to be shorter than segment CD (Fig. 7.10, right), some authors argue that these segments automatically generate the depth cues frequently observed on a daily basis (Fig. 7.11). Indeed, this illusion would be less pronounced with non-occidental populations less accustomed to the architecture made of many angles and squares as is often the cases in Western countries.

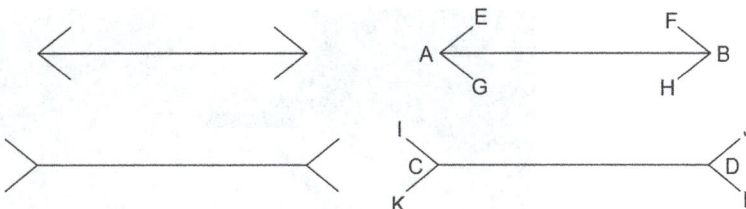

Fig. 7.10 The Müller-Lyer illusion (on the *left*), where the *horizontal line, bottom part*, seems longer than the *top left horizontal line*; letters on the illustration on the *right* serve an explanation reported in the text

Fig. 7.11 These cabinets contain clues reminding the Müller-Lyer illusion. The two *long vertical black lines* appear to be of equal length. However, the one on the *right* is shorter by about 15 %. Indeed, the two *vertical lines* are not placed in the same context. Even by adding the length of the wooden parts just below and just above the line on the *right*, this line remains shorter than the *black line* on the *left*

Other illusions are essentially based on perspective effects. A simple case is that of the Ponzo illusion (Fig. 7.12). Also, it is possible to create a variant of this illusion with the railroad track illustration used earlier and the addition on the picture of same size segments at different locations on the track. If the size of the segments is not adjusted for perspective, the highest segment appears longer, and the lowest segment appears shorter.

A spectacular case involving a perspective effect is that of the Ames room. This room is not square as would suggest our knowledge of what a normal room is. It rather has a side (the photo in Fig. 7.13) deeper and higher than the other. A major visual distortion can happen when looking at persons in such a room. If we pay attention at the relative size of the two persons, one on the left and the other on the right, and if we assume they are in a normal environment (in which one would think they are at the same distance from us as would spontaneously suggest normal size

Fig. 7.12 Illustration of
the Ponzo illusion

constancy mechanisms), the person on the right looks oversized compared to the
person on the left. Also if one person was to move along the back wall, the size of
that person would change: the person on the right would shrink if going left, and the
one on the left would grow if going right.

There are other ways of generating strong illusions. One of them is to take images
of different sizes close to each other and to compare them. Among the illusions of
this kind, those of Delboeuf and of Titchener (Fig. 7.14) are noteworthy. Another
classic illusion is the Oppel-Kundt: a segment divided into several parts is perceived
to be longer than a segment of equal length but undivided (Fig. 7.15).

The length of a segment also depends on its orientation. Thus, a segment of a
given length appears longer vertically than horizontally (Fig. 7.16). According to
Künnapas, who wrote a series of articles about this illusion in the 1950s (see
Prinzmetal & Gettleman, 1993), a frame effect is causing the illusion. Because the
visual field is elliptical, a vertical segment is closer than a horizontal segment of the
same length to the frame (i.e., closer to the ends of the visual field). Coren and
Girgus (1978) rather hypothesized that the vertical appears longer because it
involves a depth cue and the horizontal does not. If you are asked to indicate the
midpoint of a vertical line, you will probably not indicate a location dividing the
line in two equal parts, but a point located a bit higher than midpoint because higher
means farther away (more distance).

7.3.2   The Moon Illusion

Because of its ubiquity and also because it has intrigued philosophers and scientists
for a long time, the moon illusion deserves we spend some time on it. This illusion
is so strong that we forget or even doubt that it is an illusion. This illusion is even
more interesting that a plausible explanation requires the perfect integration of the

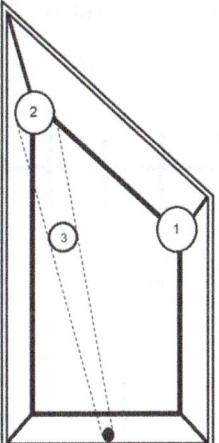

Fig. 7.13 The effect generated when two people are in the Ames room (photo on *top*). Below, a bird's-eye view of the room. If an observer (*black dot*) believes that *person 2* is at *position 3*, i.e., at the same distance as *person 1*, as suggested by the depth cues in the room, then the observer will perceive *person 2* as much smaller because the retinal size of the latter is much smaller than that of *person 1*

fundamental notion of perceptual constancy. But what is the moon illusion? This illusion refers to the fact that the moon appears larger when it is on the horizon than when it is at its highest point in the sky (the zenith). This difference is estimated at approximately 30%, but may be sometimes smaller, sometimes much greater, depending on the exact conditions of testing and on the observers.

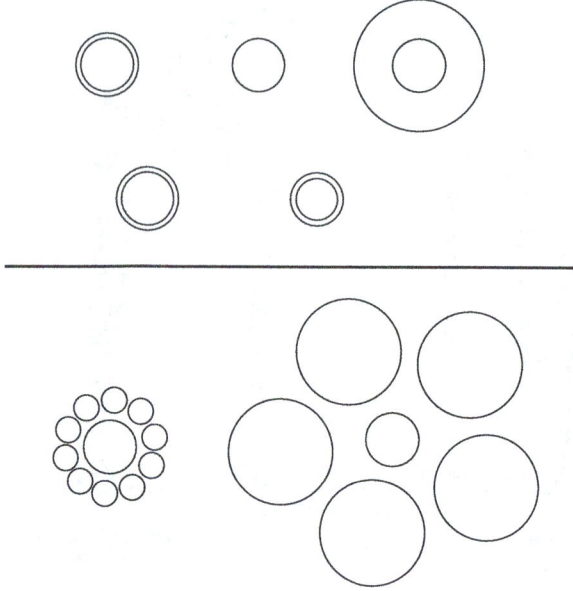

Fig. 7.14 Illustration of the Delboeuf (*top*) and Titchener (*below*) illusions

Fig. 7.15 Illustration of the Oppel-Kundt illusion. The distances between *1* and *2* and between *2* and *3* are the same although the distance between *2* and *3* seems larger

Fig. 7.16 Illustrations of the *horizontal-vertical* illusion. Is the wizard hat (*left*) wider than is tall or taller than is wide? Or does height and width seem almost equal? Just measure it! On the *right*, do *horizontal* and *vertical lines* have equal length?

Since the distance that separates us from the moon remains pretty much equivalent regardless of where it is located, its projective size remains the same, whether at the zenith or horizon. According to Irvin Rock and Lloyd Kaufman (Kaufman & Rock, 1962; Rock & Kaufman, 1962), the illusion is not caused by the different angles of the observer's gaze, as some researchers believed until then, but to the presence or absence of objects (the ground) between the observer and the moon. Rock and Kaufman rather emphasized the importance of apparent distance, also referred to as the size-distance invariance hypothesis.

In order to understand this explanation, it is crucial to remember the idea of perceptual constancy: if two objects have the same retinal size, the one that appears farther away is perceived as larger. What would happen would the brain believe that the moon is farther when on the horizon than at its zenith? Because we know that the retinal image is the same in both cases, we must conclude that the brain would interpret that the moon is larger on the horizon. In other words, we believe that the moon is very large on the horizon because our brain believes it is far away. This may seem counterintuitive for someone concluding that the moon appears to be so close because it looks so big. A full understanding requires that you keep in mind the fact we are dealing with perceptual mechanisms engaged automatically or unconsciously by the brain.

The critical question at this point becomes the following one: are there at least reasons to believe that the moon seems farther away on the horizon than at the zenith? The answer is yes, according to Kaufman and Rock. Consider the following experiment where observers were asked to point out the midpoint between the zenith, 90°, and the horizon, 0°. Rather than pointing the midpoint, which is 45°, these observers rather tended to point a direction a little closer to the horizon than to the zenith. As shown in Fig. 7.17, observers do not point to the midpoint of a sky that would be perceived as semicircular; they point rather to what is midpoint of a sky perceived as being flattened. If the sky is perceived as being flat, the moon is necessarily perceived as more distant when on the horizon than at the zenith.

There is a second reason to believe that the moon seems farther away on the horizon than at the zenith. It is recognized that the perceptual system is sensitive to

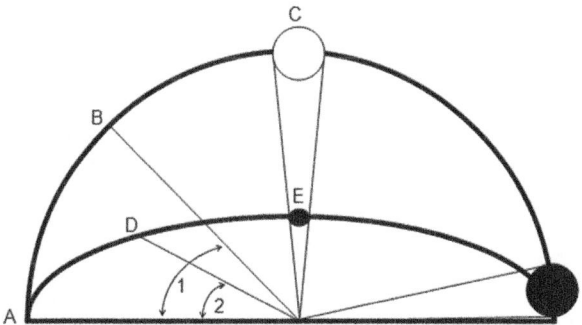

Fig. 7.17 When asking observers to indicate midpoint between the horizon and zenith, they do not indicate Point B (a 45° angle; see digit 1 in the figure); they point rather in the direction of Point D (angle 2). Point B is midpoint between A and C, C (*large white disk*) indicating the real location of the moon, D being midpoint between A and E, and E (the *small black dot*) being where the observer believes the moon is. To an observer, indicating midpoint corresponds to pointing D, assuming that the sky is perceived as being flat rather than *semicircular*. The moon is therefore judged as being closer (Point E) when standing at the zenith than when located at the horizon (the *large black disk*) (Kaufman & Rock, 1962)

the presence of benchmarks in the environment. With more landmarks ahead of us, we tend to perceive distances as larger. When looking at the moon at its zenith, there are no landmarks to guide the estimation of distance; however, most often the land offers several landmarks such as trees, cars, or houses. These landmarks help give the brain the impression that the moon on the horizon is far away from us.

In short, the moon would be perceived as being larger on the horizon than at the zenith because the brain would believe it is farther on the horizon. This explanation makes sense only if one understands the idea of perceptual constancy, that is, the principle stating that perceived distance and projective size are closely connected when estimating the size of objects. Many explanations and descriptions about the moon illusion can be found in Hershenson (1989) or Ross and Plug (2002):

> The fact that landmarks contribute to perceiving depth led to a basic rule of water safety. If you capsize a boat after moving far from the shore of a lake, be careful before deciding to swim back rather than trying to grab the boat. Because there are usually no benchmarks in the water (sometimes an island, sometimes other boats), you might get the incorrect impression of still being close to shore. Inadequate assessment of distance may cause exhaustion before reaching the shore.

Chapter 8
Perception and Attention

This final chapter is dedicated to the study of attention because perception cannot be reduced to the sole detection of stimuli. It is necessary to try to understand how what is already in the brain determines or influences what is going to be perceived. This influence was already noted on several occasions in the preceding chapters: when Helmholtz' hypothesis about unconscious inferences was referred to, or when studying form recognition or Gestalt's organization principles for accounting for visual or auditory perception.

Just for providing some idea of the impact of attention on perception, one should consider the following facts. There exists a scientific society, the Psychonomic Society, dedicated to experimental psychology and founded in the USA in 1959. This society is responsible (now with Springer) for the publication of several scientific journals. One of these journals, *Perception and Psychophysics*, was founded in the 1960s. Dedicated to research in the fields of perception and psychophysics, the journal kept the same name until 2008. Since 2009, the journal's name is *Attention, Perception, and Psychophysics*. Indeed, in 1988, 5 % of articles published in the journal were associated somehow to the study of attention; 20 years later, it was close to 50 %. Given that no important scientific journal had the word attention in its name, it has been decided to change P&P's name in order to better reflect its content. Indeed, this situation illustrates to what extent the processes linked to attention are crucial when perceiving and for understanding the mechanisms of perception.

For studying attention, it is imperative to look at its main properties. Any tentative for presenting the properties of attention will likely be incomplete given the huge amount of studies on this topic. Although the study of the attentional mechanism founded on neuroscientific approaches increased considerably in the past 30 years (see Gazzaniga, Ivry, & Mangun, 2009), the present chapter proposes only an overview of the main concepts linked to the study of attention offered by the behavioral studies and developed in cognitive psychology in the past 60 years.

© Springer International Publishing Switzerland 2016
S. Grondin, *Psychology of Perception*, DOI 10.1007/978-3-319-31791-5_8

8.1   What Is Attention?

Attention is the process allowing to become aware of a few things and to capture a part, admittedly very limited, of what is going on around. Indeed, it is extremely difficult to define attention precisely, although most of us probably already know what it is. We know that when concentrating on a sound source through noise, it is possible to increase chances to capture the message targeted. Also, even when driving a car becomes an easy task, we know that it is preferable, for the sake of attention, to lower the intensity level of radio for mobilizing all resources in a situation that would suddenly become more complicated (increased traffic, uncertainty about the street, direction when arriving in a new city, etc.).

Readers: "Right now, what are you paying attention to?" Well, certainly to the text you are reading. Yet, there are probably several other things in your environment that could have captured your attention. There is probably some noise, certainly some pressure exerted by your chair on you if you are in the likely sitting position for reading, and maybe even some odors coming from the kitchen. Before reading the last sentence, none of these possibilities was striking you; none captured your attention. Even so, as soon as you read about it, you asked yourself about the potential noise in the environment, and maybe you have identified more than one source of noise. As well, you have not been thinking about an iron or a mouse, but for having read these words, one or the other or even both probably occurred in your mind. That is attention. There is continuously a large amount of information at the reach of mind, or because our sensory systems give access to it, or because the information is already there, in memory.

Sometimes, stimuli from the environment capture attention; in such cases, we are talking about bottom-up processing (or data-driven processing). Sometimes, we decide to pay attention to something, which is referred to as a top-down process (concept-driven processing).

8.1.1   Blindnesses

There are two types of errors, now classic in psychology, issued from the scientific literature on attention. They are called blindness. One is change blindness and refers to the difficulty that people may have to detect what could be quite a big change on an object that is part of a scene that is being observed. Indeed, the difficulty to detect a change, for instance, from one image to another one that looks like the first one, when the presentation of these two images is alternated, depends on the magnitude of change in the context of the presented image (Rensink, 2002; Rensink, O'Regan, & Clark, 1997).

Along the same line, it is sometimes difficult to note the presence of new objects, or of new stimuli, occurring in a scene. This last case is called attentional blindness. As for change blindness, attentional blindness occurs when too much attention is allocated to a specific part of a scene. A classic example of such effect is the one where someone is asked to count the number of passes of a ball among teammates: nearly half of the people asked to complete this relatively simple task are unable to observe the arrival of a huge stimulus, a gorilla, in the middle of the scene at some moment, through the passes between teammates. This demonstration is available on the following website: http://www.simonslab.com/videos.html.

A phenomenon like this one leads to believe that a conscious perception of the world is made possible only with the contribution of attention. Along the same line, there exist recent results showing that there is also attentional deafness, i.e., a difficulty to detect the presence of an auditory stimulus through other auditory dynamic stimuli (Dalton & Fraenkel, 2012). Note also that a participant asked to complete a difficult visual discrimination task is susceptible to miss the presentation of an easily detectable sound presented during this visual task (Macdonald & Lavie, 2011). It is therefore possible to induce an effect of attentional deafness with the manipulation of a difficult visual task.

The next three parts of this chapter are dedicated to three important properties of attentional processes. These properties are the capability to prepare attention in space and time, for capturing more efficiently the forthcoming information; the capability to operate a selection of the information available around, be it delivered visually or auditorily; and the capability of searching for specific information in the visual field.

8.2   Preparation and Orientation

Typically, research on attention is based on an analysis of the time necessary to provide a response (response time) in specific situations (Posner, 1978). Inferences about the mechanisms at play are based on the results issuing from various experimental situations.

8.2.1   Spatial Preparation

The study of the deployment of attentional mechanisms can be made with a classic strategy where, for instance, participants are asked to direct their gaze toward a point in the center of a computer screen in front of them. The participants need to press as rapidly as possible the appropriate key (on a keyboard) when a stimulus occurs that will be delivered on the left or on the right of the central fixation point. This first step provides an idea of the time it takes to do such a simple detection task. In a next step, a cue (for instance, a little arrow pointing in the left or in the right direction) occurs at the fixation point, indicating where the stimulus will be presented. Here, we are talking about a spatial cue. Generally, conditions are generated where the cue is valid 80% of the time; in the other 20%, the cue is misleading. With such an experimental manipulation, it is possible to show that the valid cue allows a reduction of the response time; however, a nonvalid cue has the opposite effect, and, consequently, the time taken to hit the appropriate key is increased. Also, note that if the cue and the stimulus are presented simultaneously, there is no effect. Moreover, the cueing effect increases when the duration between the presentation of the cue and the presentation of the stimulus (*stimulus onset asynchrony*— SOA) is increased; this improvement continues up to an SOA lasting 150 ms.

Such experiments show that it is possible to prepare the attentional mechanisms for increasing efficiency in a task where a stimulus presented at different spatial locations has to be detected. It is as if it is possible to shift attention from one place to another, just like a light beam can be moved. Researchers sometimes refer to attentional spotlight and talk about attentional displacement. We do not really know if, strictly speaking, the spotlight moving is the best analogy for describing this attentional mechanism. One can rather imagine a lens with which it is possible to focus, on a point of fixation, but that would allow an enlargement of the field in such a way that it would become possible to include stimuli located on the left and on the right.

That said, there exists a phenomenon called the *inhibition of return*. Anticipating the presence of an event at a certain location allows detecting it more rapidly and with more accuracy. This inhibition of return refers to the difficulty to send attention back at the spatial location where attention was actually maintained during a brief period (Klein, 2000). More specifically, the original demonstration, by Posner and Cohen (1984), goes as follows.

Let a visual set with a central fixation point and another point located on each side where there may appear a signal. A participant has to react as rapidly as possible to the occurrence of this signal. If a cue is first given, with the illumination of one of the two points on each side, for indicating where the signal will appear, the participant takes less time to react to the occurrence of the signal if it appears at the predicted location than if it appears on the opposite side. That is a facilitation effect. Note that over the series of trials, there are catch trials where the cue is misleading. Thus, the participant cannot anticipate because this would cause an increase of false alarms and therefore a decrease of precision level.

The facilitation effect, measured with the difference of reaction time to the signal target according to the fact that the signal occurs where the cue was located or on the opposite side, is observed however only if the time difference between the arrival of the cue and the arrival of the signal target is very small (from 0 to 100 ms). With a 200-ms difference, reaction time is about the same, whether the target stimulus is presented on the same side as the cue or on the opposite side (Fig. 8.1). But when this difference is increased, the results become quite fascinating. With a 300- to 500-ms difference between the cue and target, it takes less time to react to the signal target if it is presented on the side opposite to the one where the cue occurred. These results are explained by the fact that attention was oriented toward a precise location and then disengaged from this location. This orientation and the disengagement prevent a new engagement of attention at the original location. Some researchers claim that this inhibition of return is due to the involvement of mechanisms responsible for eye movement (Rafal, Calabresi, Brennan, & Sciolto, 1989).

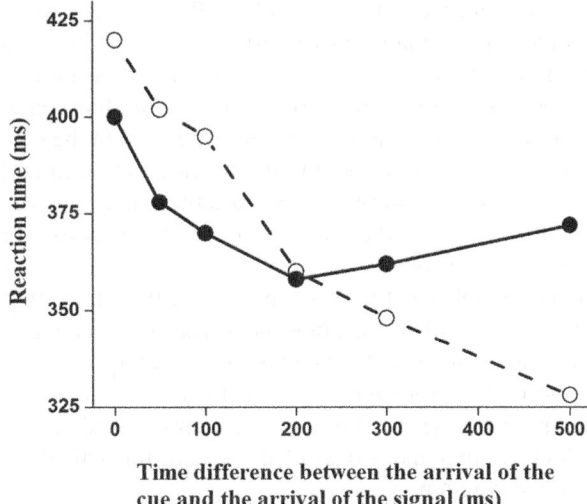

Fig. 8.1 Results from Posner and Cohen (1984) showing the *inhibition-of-return* effect; *black dots*, target with cues; *white dots*, target without cue

8.2.2   Temporal Preparation

Just like it is possible to be prepared to shift attention as a function of the arrival of a stimulus in space, it is possible to be prepared for the arrival of a stimulus at a given moment in time. So it is possible to learn to read the links between events in order to get ready at the moment something occurs. Reading the warning signs allows to increasing the efficiency of the response to give. For instance, when driving a car, the occurrence of a yellow light (in North America) means that one should be prepared to stop.

Once again, one can use the response time to study how we prepare in time. It is important to understand that a simple task such as responding to the arrival of a signal requires the contribution of a series of processing steps. The stimulus must be detected and identified; the appropriate response must be chosen; and the motor programming that the response requires has to be engaged. In this context, the preparation means to try to do in advance what is preceding the response. In the following description, we will stick to cases involving simple reaction times (Niemi & Näätänen, 1981).

Thus, a typical experiment for studying this preparation is to use a warning signal before the presentation of a target stimulus to which a participant must react as quickly as possible. This signal can reduce the uncertainty related to the moment of occurrence of the target stimulus. After the appearance of the warning signal, the more time passes, the more the arrival of the target stimulus becomes likely. This information alone has the effect of reducing the reaction time when the stimulus occurs. The interval between the warning signal and the target stimulus is called the preparatory period. This period allows being oriented in time.

The effect of temporal preparation depends on the specific experimental conditions under which a participant has to perform. We can carry out blocks of trials where the preparatory period remains the same (constant condition) or vary the duration of this period from trial to trial (variable condition), using periods identical to what is used in the constant condition. In the constant condition, the longer the preparatory period, the slower the reaction time (Bausenhart, Rolke, & Ulrich, 2008). In contrast in the variable condition, the longer the preparatory period, the shorter the reaction time. This applies to all kinds of durations of preparatory periods.

This effect, in the variable condition, is explained by the following principle: the more time passes, the more likely becomes the arrival of the target stimulus, and, consequently, one tends to increase the preparation according to this probability. In the constant condition, the probability is fixed; there is no change of likelihood being tested. One probably needs to rely on the simple calculation of the period preceding the stimulus, after the arrival of the signal, this calculation involving more variability as the duration increases.

8.3   Selectivity

Since a multitude of environmental stimuli constantly reach our sensory receptors, there is, within our reach, a wealth of information. What is brought to consciousness depends on where the focus is. It is not possible to hear everything and see everything at the same time. We must somehow choose and this choice is made through attentional selectivity. It is possible to focus on a specific source of information. For example, all students know that it is possible to simulate listening in class, but actually watching from the corner of the eye (to direct attention to) another person of the class! Similarly, it is not because the person in front of you looks at you in the eye at a dinner at the restaurant that he or she is not trying to follow the conversation at the next table! In the following paragraphs, we will describe how the study of selectivity in different sensory modalities, visual and auditory, is conducted.

8.3.1   Visual Selectivity

The stimuli reaching the retina are not only numerous, but they sometimes succeed at a high speed, when reading, for example, or when looking outside by the side window when moving by car. Also, as we have seen when studying the perception of form, the trace left by the stimuli on the retina persists for some time. Playing with the selectivity of attentional processes, it is possible to investigate the duration and the properties of this information on the retina.

The technique of partial report, developed by George Sperling, allows studying these properties. Let us consider the following situation. A series of 12 letters are presented simultaneously to participants on a screen and this, during 50 ms. Those letters are arranged in three rows of four. During some trials, participants are asked to report as many letters as they can. Generally, in such conditions (full report), participants will report four or five letters. The question that arises is why are there only four or five of the 12 letters that are recalled? One answer may lie on the fact that we can capture no more than four or five letters at the same time, which would reveal some perceptual limit in our way of capturing information. Another explanation could be the following one. Maybe all the information (the 12 letters) is available for a short time, but while the first letters are recalled, the others disappear.

It is in order to test this second explanation that Sperling (1960) has developed his clever strategy, the partial report. This technique is based on the idea of a pairing between a sound and a row of letters. Thus, high-, medium-, and low-frequency sounds are associated with the rows of four letters from the top, middle, and bottom, which is the 12-letter set on the screen. Immediately after the short presentation of letters, a sound is presented to the participant. This sound indicates which letters, specifically, should be reported. If the sound is most acute (high frequency), one must report the letters arranged on the top row. If the failure to report more than four or five letters, on average, in a global report is related to a limit on the number of letters perceived, one should report only one or two letters per row, on average, during the partial report. However, if all the information is available for a brief period before the information is erased, one should report more than one or two letters per row, on average.

It appears that during the partial report, participants are much better. They can report on average at least three letters per row. In other words, the information is there for a short time, and, if one directs attention immediately to the information, we have access to it. It is important to specify that the sound is presented only after the presentation of the letters is completed. This means that participants cannot direct in advance their attention on a row.

It is when the sound signal is presented immediately at the end of the visual presentation that the partial report shows the most benefits (more letters recalled on average). In fact, Sperling has shown that the introduction of a gap between the end of the presentation of the letters and the sound nullified the benefits associated with the partial report. With an interval of 150 or even 300 ms, more letters are reminded on average than with a global report, but this effect disappears completely if the delay lasts 1 s. In short, the information is really there, available, but only for a short period.

In terms of cognitive psychology, we call sensory register—a kind of very short-term memory—the initial stage of information processing where this information persists for a short period after the disappearance of the physical stimulus. The neural activity does not stop with the end of a stimulus; it stretches slightly over time (Di Lollo & Bischof, 1995; Loftus & Irwin, 1998; Nisly & Wasserman, 1989). Sometimes the term iconic memory is used for referring to the sensory register in the visual modality (as opposed to the echoic memory for auditory modality).

In addition, another property of attentional processes that may affect the ability to perceive is called the attentional blink (Dux & Marois, 2009; Martensa & Wybleb, 2010). We can demonstrate this effect using a procedure where there are presented successively, in one place, a series of visual stimuli rather than deploying stimuli at different locations on the retina. If one asks a participant to report the presence of a digit through a series of letters presented rapidly, this participant will succeed without difficulty if the stimuli are not presented too quickly. For example, if the participant is presented with eight to ten items per second, the task will be completed with success and without too much difficulty. If asked to detect a letter of a given color, rather than a number, the participant will once again make it without difficulty. However, if asked to detect two targets, for example, a letter of a given color and a digit, the ability to detect the second target will depend on how long before the first target was presented. If the second target comes between 200 and 500 ms after the presentation of the first target, the performance is affected. In fact, this reduction occurs only if the first target has been detected. Performance will be particularly affected if the second target arrives from 200 to 300 ms after the first. The attentional blink phenomenon is exactly this difficulty to detect the second target, after having paid attention to a first target. The attention required for the processing of the first target would not be available for the processing of the second.

It is important to note that if the second target occurs about 100 ms after the first, there will be no decrease of the ability to capture the second, as if both targets could be captured together, before the blink. In brief, this attentional blink phenomenon teaches the deployment over time of processes linked to selective attention.

8.3.2   Auditory Selectivity

When one pays attention to a precise source of information, what other information available in the environment can be captured? Is it possible to extract anything else? Yes, probably. For instance, during celebrations in a room where there are multiple conversations in parallel, it is usually possible to follow efficiently the conversation where the attention is directed at. Although it is not possible to follow another conversation, it is likely that you will react if someone around mentions your name.

Researchers interested in attentional selectivity often used a procedure called dichotic listening. In a dichotic-listening task, a participant hears through headphones two messages at a time, one in each ear. The experimenter asks a participant to follow specifically the message sent to one ear, the left or the right one, and to ignore the other. The participant is asked to repeat aloud the message that is followed, just to make sure that it is actually well followed.

The work by Cherry (1953) indicates that there is a minimum of information coming from the ear receiving no attention that remains available. The participant is able to determine if, in this ear, a voice was heard, and when it is actually a voice, it is possible to extract some physical features (for instance, was it a low or high voice), but not to understand the meaning of the message. Also, if a series of digits are delivered simultaneously in each ear and no priority for left or right ear is assigned to participants, they will report information coming from both ears, not in a chronological order of arrival, but ear by ear.

This type of studies raises the question about the level where attention plays a role in the sequence of information processing. Broadbent (1958) proposed the idea that there exists an attentional filter, a kind of Y-shaped tube that can only let a limited quantity of information passing through. Indeed, according to this researcher, a central information processing system is responsible for the reception of information from different sensory channels for eventually determining the meaning on the basis of what is already stored in memory. By letting only stimuli having some specific features to enter, the filter would serve to avoid an overload of work to this central system. The filter does not allow shifting from one channel to another. If that would be the case, it would become possible to listen to more than one conversation at a time. The selectivity would then operate early, i.e., at the level of acoustical features. Therefore, the selectivity of information would occur at a low level, before any semantic analysis would be made.

Following Broadbent's findings, studies like the ones by Gray and Wedderburn (1960) showed that the attentional filter would rather operate a late selection. In one study, participants heard simultaneously in each ear, for instance, messages like the following ones:

In the left ear	Hy—2—gen
In the right ear	6—dro—9

It was therefore possible to hear simultaneously "Hy 6," "2 dro," and "gen 9." When participants were asked to follow what is reported in the left ear, to ignore what is reported in the right ear, and then to report what was heard, they reported "Hy-dro-gen." In other words, participants' attention was shifted from one ear to the other and this, as a function of the meaning of the words. In brief, if it was once thought that the attentional selection was made rapidly in the information processing sequence, it was henceforth necessary to believe that selection occurs at an ulterior stage of processing given that there must have been some understanding of the meaning for explaining the shifting from one ear to the other in Gray and Wedderburn's study.

Anne Treisman also used dichotic listening, but rather presented segments of sentences in each ear. Once again, the results showed that participants follow the meaning of the message from one ear to the other, rather than to stick with the task requiring to following what is sent to one ear specifically. These results support the idea that there is a late filter (see Deutsch & Deutsch, 1963) or, in the terms of Treisman (1960), the idea that it would rather be an attenuator instead of a filter.

Instead of searching for the location of the filter or attenuator in the information processing sequence, researchers in the field of attention eventually preferred to emphasize the distinction between automatic processes and processes based on controlled attention (Johnston & Dark, 1986). Generally speaking, this approach shows a concern for attentional capacities, i.e., for the distribution of attentional resources in different tasks. This approach goes far beyond the scope of the present book, which is focused on perceptual processes. Attentional resources being limited, researchers in this study field wanted to know the mental load of different cognitive tasks, to what extent these tasks solicit or not the same resources, and how these tasks can reach some automaticity. Nowadays, in a society where everyone seems to search for time to the point of combining tasks like using a cell phone and driving a car, it is easy to understand the importance of knowing the attentional load imposed by tasks (Strayer & Johnston, 2001).

Being exposed to the Stroop effect rapidly provides an idea of what the automatic activation of a process looks like (MacLeod, 1991; Stroop, 1935). This effect appears when one tries to name the color with which each word is written, each word designating a color actually. It is very difficult to ignore the meaning of the word (the color designated when reading) when trying to simply name the color used to write the word. Reading is not required in this task; just naming the color is required. Nevertheless, reading imposes itself automatically and, consequently, causes interference. Just to catch the strength of this effect, go to Fig. 8.2 and try see

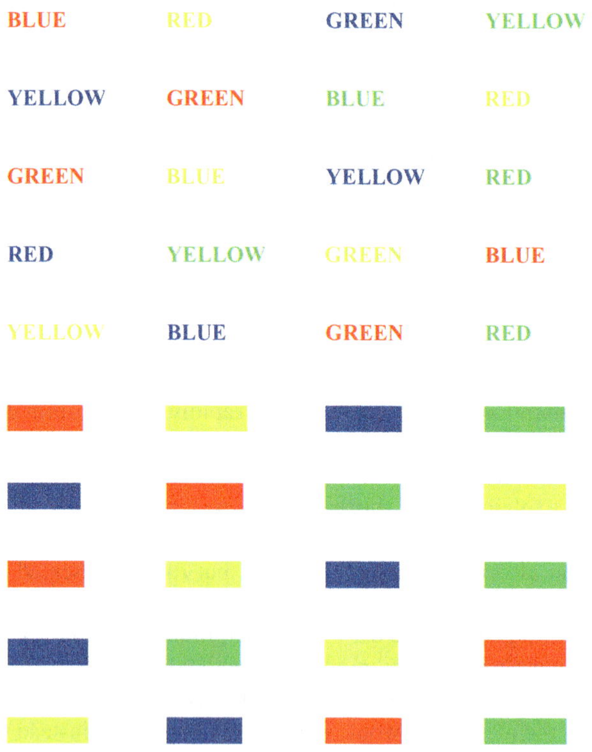

Fig. 8.2 Example of a Stroop effect. Naming the color (*lower set*) of each of the 20 *rectangles* (five rows of four colors) takes much less time than naming the color (*upper set*) used for writing each of the words. This demonstration illustrates an interference effect caused by the automatic activation of word reading

how much time you need for naming each color in the lower series (colors without letters). Then, see how much time it takes for naming each color in the upper series (colors with letters). There should quite a large difference (several seconds). You may also try to simply read each word of the series of words. Once again, you should observe that it takes much less time to complete this task than it takes to name the colors in the same series.

8.4   Visual Search

The tasks used in the preceding part of the chapter on attentional selectivity are somewhat artificial. For instance, in the case of visual selectivity, participants are asked in advance where to look. In everyday life, one rather needs to search actively for something in a set of stimuli. Indeed, being able to extract visually something from the environment does not rely on the sole stimulation of the retina. When several elements are at the reach of sight, one has to search for a specific item for seeing it (Wolfe & Horowitz, 2004).

A part of the study of attentional mechanisms is dedicated to visual search. Typical tasks to complete in this research field involve the presentation of a series of items to a participant who is asked to find a specific item (a target).

In an experiment where a letter must be found among many others, the specific features of these letters will determine how easy or difficult it is to spot the target letter. Figure 8.3 illustrates visual sets like the ones used by Neisser (1964). It is much easier to detect letter Z in the left set given the numerous features Z shares with letters in the right set.

There are cases where the number of items determines the time needed for detecting a target and cases where this number has no impact. For instance, in Fig. 8.4, it is possible to detect rapidly, in the upper set (five letters), letter Z or even both letters O. However, spotting Z in the lower left set is much easier than spotting O in the lower right set. Indeed, increasing the number of items in conditions like the one in the lower right set results in longer time for detecting the target letter (O). However, increasing the number of items (O or Q) in the left set would not change the time needed to detect letter Z: the target simply pops out. It is the fact that a target shares more or less features with other items that determines the possibility that a target pops out or not.

Researchers have also been interested in visual search of features besides the strict letter framework. Different features were used like rectangles being presented horizontally or vertically or presented in different colors. Usually, participants are asked to detect a target on the basis of only one feature. Sometimes, the task gets a little more complicated, as in a conjunction search where participants are asked to detect a target involving at least two types of features.

A classic explanation of the functioning of visual search is the feature integration theory (Treisman & Gelade, 1980). This theory of visual attention is based on the idea that processing an object or a visual scene involves two steps. First, at a preattentive

Fig. 8.3 Example of visual sets used by Neisser (1964)	

	ODUGQR	IVMXEW
	QCDUGO	EWVMIX
	CQOGRD	EXWMVI
	QUGCDR	IXEMWV
	URDGQO	VXWEMI
	GRUQDO	MXVEWI
	DUZGRO	XVWMEI
	UCGROD	MWXVIE
	DQRCGU	VIMEXW
	QDOCGU	EXVWIM
	CGUROQ	VWMIEX
	OCDURQ	VMWIEX
	UOCGQD	XVWMEI
	RGQCOU	WXVEMI
	GRUDQO	XMEWIV
	GODUCQ	MXIVEW
	QCURDO	VEWMIX
	DUCOQG	EMVXWI
	CGRDQU	IVWMEX
	UDRCOQ	IEVMWX
	GQCORU	WVZMXE
	GOQUCD	XEMIWV
	GDQUOC	WXIMEV
	URDCGO	EMWIVX
	GODRQC	IVEMXW

stage, an object is processed as a function of its features. It is then possible to proceed to the analysis of a certain number of features because they are processed in parallel, i.e., in an automatic way, without the contribution of attentional resources. The theory also posits a second stage where it is necessary to link features to objects: that is referred to as the *binding* problem (Treisman, 1996). This processing stage requires attentional resources, attention being directed toward one item at a time. The idea that there exist two processing stages, i.e., that there are, on the one hand, features per se constituting an object and, on the other hand, a need to link these features, is supported by what is observed when participants are placed in very difficult conditions. Presenting illusory conjunctions generates such difficult conditions (Treisman & Schmidt, 1982). These illusory conjunctions are errors occurring when one reports having seen, in a visual set, a letter of a certain color. This letter was presented, and the color reported too, but this exact letter in this exact color was not presented.

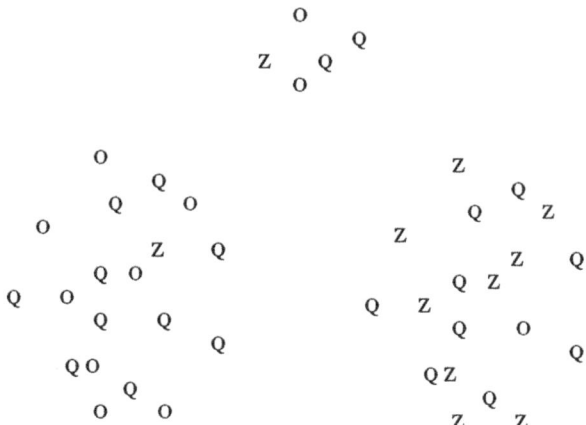

Fig. 8.4 If one searches for letter Z in a stimulus set like the one on the *lower left part*, the size of the visual set has no impact; however, if one searches letter O in a stimulus set like the one on the *lower right part*, the size of the set becomes critical. In the former case, Z emerges spontaneously (pop-out phenomenon)

8.5 Clinical Aspects

There exist different attentional problems having impact on perception. One of these is called hemineglect. Someone suffering from parietal cortex damage might well experience problems with visual attention. More specifically, if a lesion is on the right cerebral hemisphere, the patient will not be able to pay attention to all material located on the contralateral (opposite) side, i.e., to anything located at the left of a fixation point. A special case of hemineglect is called extinction. A patient with such a deficit would be able to see an object located on the contralateral side, but only if there is no object at the corresponding location in the other visual hemi-field (i.e., on the ipsilateral side).

Sometimes, parietal lesions can be bilateral. In these rare cases, a patient suffers from a problem called the Balint syndrome. Different symptoms may result from this problem. For instance, a patient seems able to see only one object at the time. It is as if everything around the object one is paying attention to simply does not exist anymore. This incapacity to perceive more than a single object at a time is some-times referred to as simultagnosia.

Finally, there are cases where, following cerebral lesions, patients report being unable to see some objects (Weiskrantz, 1986). However, they do "guess correctly" their location if one insists for having them pointing where they are. This phenom-enon, called *blindsight*, reveals the fact that it does not look necessary to consciously see something for acting or reacting to this thing.

Appendix A: ROC Curves

The *receiver operating characteristic* (ROC) curves are used to capture at a glance both the level of discrimination (d') and the decision criterion (for instance, β). An ROC curve is obtained when plotting the probabilities of a hit, on the ordinate, and the probabilities of a false alarm, on the abscissa (Fig. A.1).

The sensitivity of an observer will be revealed by the distance of the curve from the diagonal, which represents the case where $d'=0$. Furthermore, the observer's response bias is revealed by the location of a point on a given curve. The performance of a lax observer, i.e., of someone with a high rate of hits and false alarms, is represented by a point in the upper right of the curve, whereas the performance of a conservative observer is represented by a point in the lower left.

There are specific ways to move the decision criterion of an observer, i.e., to change the location of a point on a given ROC curve. One of these ways is to assign rewards (e.g., giving participant money) for each hit and to administer punishment (asking participant for money) for each false alarm. Depending on the value of rewards and punishments, the observer will adjust the criterion. If there is more money involved for a hit than for a false alarm, the observer will adopt a lax criterion (the point will move up and to the right on the ROC curve). Conversely, observers will become much more conservative in their way of making decisions in conditions where it is necessary to pay more for a false alarm than what could be obtained for a hit. It is important to remind that the movements of the criterion do not affect sensitivity.

Note in conclusion that the ROC curves are also used to test some assumptions underlying the signal detection theory. For example, with the transformation of proportions into Z-scores, it becomes possible to determine whether the distribution noise and signal + noise are normal and whether their variance is the same. In the first case (normal distributions), for a given ROC curve transformed into Z-scores, the points should fall on or near the linear function, and in the second case (equal variance assumption), the slope of this function should be 1.

© Springer International Publishing Switzerland 2016
S. Grondin, *Psychology of Perception*, DOI 10.1007/978-3-319-31791-5

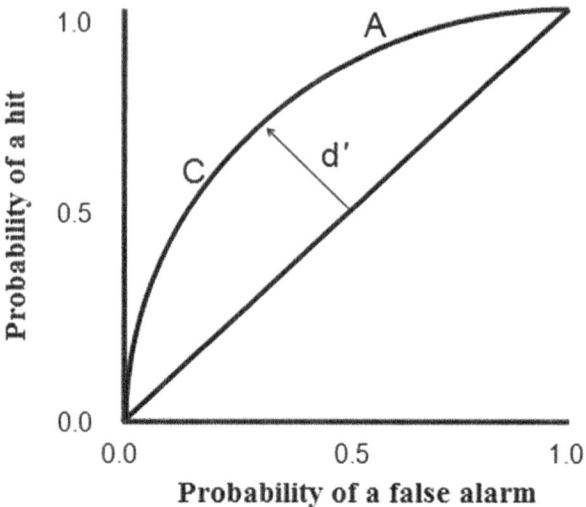

Fig. A.1 On this *receiver operating characteristic* (ROC) curve, sensitivity (d') is the same everywhere. C is a conservative observer and A is a lax observer. C and A would therefore have a different criterion

Appendix B: Fechner's Law

Founder of psychophysics, Gustav Fechner was interested in the nature of the relationship between the magnitude of a stimulus and the magnitude of sensation. Fechner believed that this relationship was bound to be logarithmic. Indeed, to establish the relationship, he postulated that the magnitude of the sensation can be described by a unit called the just-noticeable difference (JND), which itself could be quantified indirectly on the basis of the Weber fraction. The 0 point of his psychological scale is the absolute threshold.

Thus, for a sensory continuum having an absolute threshold equal to 10 (arbitrary units) and a Weber fraction of 0.3, the calculation of the scale is as follows:

JND	Value (in log)
$1 = 10 + (10 \times 0.3) = 13$	(1.114)
$2 = 13 + (13 \times 0.3) = 16.9$	(1.228)
$3 = 16.9 + (16.9 \times 0.3) = 21.97$	(1.342)
$4 = 21.97 + (21.97 \times 0.3) = 28.56$	(1.456)
$5 = 28.56 + (28.56 \times 0.3) = 37.13$	(1.570)
$6 = 37.13 + (37.13 \times 0.3) = 48.27$	(1.684)
And so on	

In short, to achieve a JND, the stimulus in this example must have a value of 13. The next JND occurs when the intensity is 16.9. Reported graphically, these values show that the relationship between JND, on the y-axis, and the value of stimuli, on the x-axis, increases logarithmically (Fig. B.1, left). If it is rather the logarithmic value of stimuli that is used on the x-axis, the relationship becomes linear (Fig. B.1, right).

This logarithmic relationship can be summarized in the following equation:

$$JND = K \log \phi$$

where JND is the sensation, K is a multiplicative constant whose value is related to a given modality and a given sensory dimension, and ϕ is the stimulus intensity above the absolute threshold.

© Springer International Publishing Switzerland 2016

S. Grondin, *Psychology of Perception*, DOI 10.1007/978-3-319-31791-5

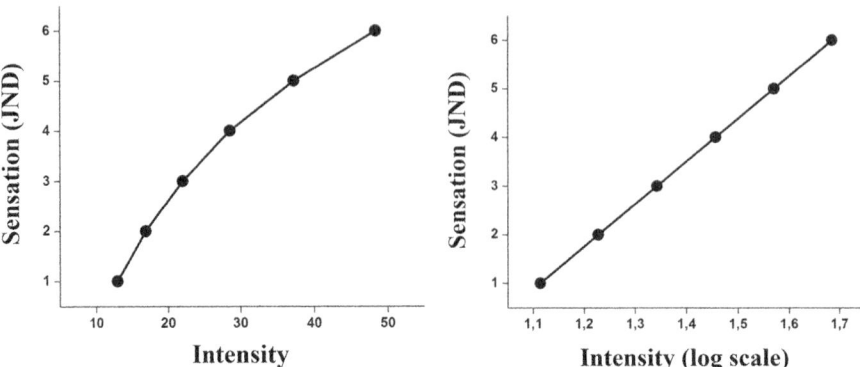

Fig. B.1 Relationship between the value of a "just-noticeable difference" (JND) and the intensity of the stimuli on the linear scale (on the *left*) and on a logarithmic (on the *right*)

In the mind of Fechner, the fourth JND corresponds to something that is psychologically twice as high as the second JND. This indirect way of establishing the link between sensation and the physical magnitude was incorrect, especially considering the fact that the Weber fraction is not constant, being higher for low physical magnitudes. The direct way in which Stevens addressed the issue of the relationship between the magnitude of a stimulus and the sensory magnitude was proved to be more fruitful.

Appendix C: The Nervous System

The study of the nervous system requires many nuances. Nevertheless, tracing the main lines of the anatomy of the nervous system should allow to develop a clear view of the link between the peripheral activity of the sensory receptors and the one occurring at higher levels of processing, that is, those that lead to the brain.

The nervous system is divided into the central nervous system and peripheral nervous system. The main parts of the central nervous system are described below. The peripheral nervous system includes the autonomic nervous system (which consists of the sympathetic and parasympathetic systems) and the somatic nervous system. The latter is particularly interesting because it includes the nerves.

C.1 Nerves

Neurons are the basic units of the nervous system because they allow the transmission of nerve impulses and therefore the transmission of the information throughout the body. The nerves are groups of axons in the peripheral nervous system, the axon of the neuron being the prolongation of cell body up to many ramifications.

The nerves are in charge of the transmission of nerve impulses from receptors to the spinal cord. The peripheral nervous system is composed of 12 pairs of cranial nerves and 31 pairs of spinal nerves. Cranial nerves, which are designated by numbers I to XII, also have a name providing information about their function. Some nerves are strictly efferent, others strictly afferent, and others, like the trigeminal (V), have both functions. In the context of the study of sensation and perception, it should be emphasized that nerves I, II, and VIII are, respectively, associated with olfaction, vision, and hearing. In the latter case, it is more specifically the vestibulo-cochlear nerve, indicating that a branch of the nerve is assigned to the vestibular system, which is located in the inner ear.

© Springer International Publishing Switzerland 2016
S. Grondin, *Psychology of Perception*, DOI 10.1007/978-3-319-31791-5

Spinal nerves are determined according to the height where they are located on the spine: cervical (1–8), thoracic (1–12), lumbar (1–5), sacral (of 1–5), and coccygeal (1) nerves. Each of these nerves innervates a band (or segmented area) of the skin called dermatome.

C.2   Central Nervous System

C.2.1   Major Divisions

The central nervous system includes the encephalon and spinal cord. The encephalon is the general term which includes the brain, brain stem, and cerebellum. Suffice it here to recall that the brain includes the cerebral cortex (or the forebrain), in addition to important structures (the limbic system, thalamus, and hypothalamus). Just below the brain is the brainstem which includes, from top to bottom, the midbrain, the pons, and the bulb. The cerebellum is located just behind the brainstem and the spinal cord is located just below the brainstem. Table C.1 summarizes the main divisions of the central nervous system.

C.2.2   Cerebral Cortex

Different areas of the cerebral cortex are specialized in specific functions. For locating these areas easily, it is useful to identify, in Fig. C.1, the central and lateral fissures (or sulcus) on the cortex, as well as the four lobes: frontal, occipital, parietal, and temporal. Just before the central fissure are the motor cortex and premotor cortex, and just behind, we find the somatosensory cortex, which is itself divided into two areas, called primary and secondary. The primary somatosensory cortex receives

Table C.1 Divisions of the central nervous system and some associated terms

Encephalon = brain + brain stem + cerebellum
Brain = cerebral cortex + limbic system + thalamus + hypothalamus
Brainstem = midbrain + pons + bulb
Telencephalon (or cerebral cortex)
Diencephalon (thalamus + hypothalamus)
Mesencephalon (or midbrain)
Metencephalon (pons)
Myelencephalon (bulb)
Forebrain = telencephalon + diencephalon
Midbrain = mesencephalon
Hindbrain = pons + bulb + cerebellum

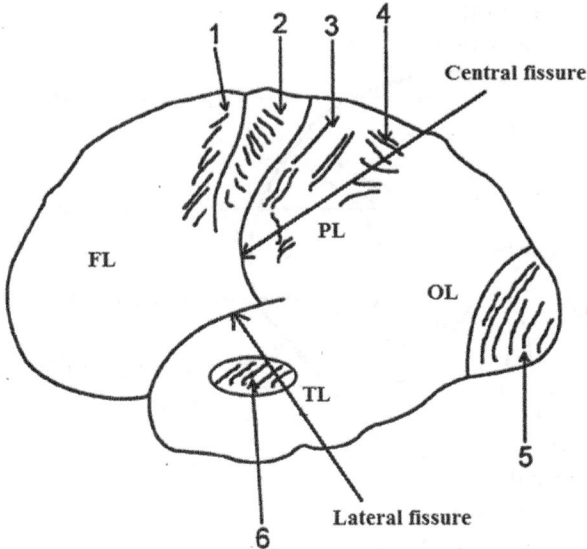

FL: Frontal Lobe PL: Parietal lobe TL: Temporal lobe OL: Occipital lobe

1. Pre-motor cortex 2. Motor cortex 3. Primary somatosensory cortex
4. Secondary somatosensory cortex 5. Visual cortex 6. Auditory cortex

Fig. C.1 Main functional areas of the cerebral cortex

information directly from the receptor organs, whereas the secondary somatosensory cortex receives only information that has previously been processed elsewhere in the brain, including in the primary somatosensory cortex. The auditory cortex is located in the temporal lobe, while the different divisions of the visual cortex are located on the back, in the occipital lobe.

C.2.3 The Spinal Cord and Sensory Pathways

The spinal cord is the part of the central nervous system, protected by the spine, which provides communication (i.e., the transmission of nerve impulses) between the peripheral nervous system and the brain and between the brain and effectors (muscles). If one makes a cross section of the spinal cord, it is possible to observe several columns which are actually groups of numerous axons. These columns are ascendant (or afferent) when assigned to the transmission of information from the periphery to the brain or descendant (or efferent) when assigned to the transmission of nerve impulses from the brain to effectors (muscles).

Figure C.2 allows to distinguish a ventral part (or anterior), toward the front, and a dorsal part (or posterior), toward the back. What is on the sides is called lateral.

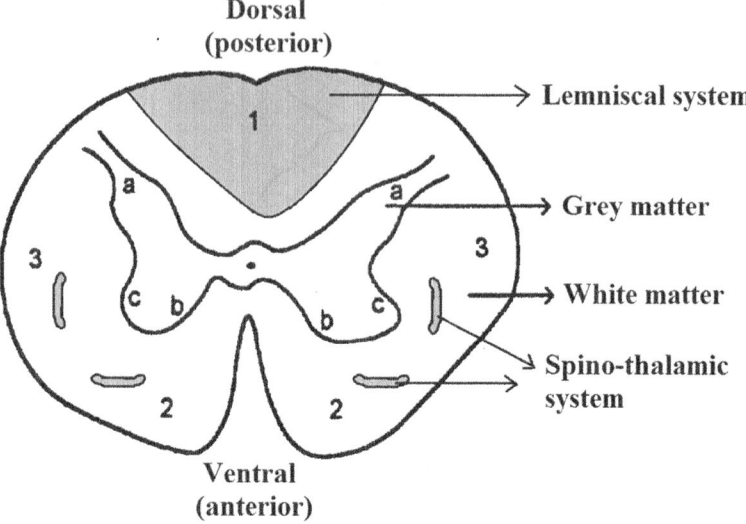

a. Posterior horn   b. Anterior horn   c. Lateral horn
1. Posterior column   2. Anterior column   3. Lateral column

Fig. C.2 Cross section of the spinal cord

This helps to identify the dorsal, ventral, or lateral horns, located in the gray matter of the spinal cord, and the dorsal, ventral, or lateral columns, located in the white matter.

There are two main pathways responsible for transmitting sensory information. Both systems differ by the exact location where there circulates the nerve impulse and by the type of information that is conveyed. To easily understand the path of the nerve impulse from the receptors to the brain receptors, it is important to remember that the information received on one side of the body, left or right, is transferred in the contralateral side, right or left, of the brain. The transfer of information from one side of the body to another sometimes occurs at the level of the spinal cord, i.e., immediately at the level where the sensation is produced. This is the case of the spinothalamic system (or extralemniscal system): information crosses from one hemibody to the other upon entry into the spinal cord and is routed directly to the thalamus where there is a relay (synapse) with another neuron. From there, the nerve impulse is sent to an area of the cerebral cortex specialized in somesthesia. At the level of the spinal cord, the influx travels though the anterolateral part.

A portion of the sensory information follows a different route to reach the somatosensory cortex. This other pathway is characterized in that the transfer of nerve impulses from one side of the body to another does not occur at the level of the spinal cord, but much higher in the nervous system, namely, at the bulb level. After crossing at the bulb, there is also a synapse, before the projection in the

Table C.2 Central pathways used for the transmission of sensory information

Spinothalamic system	Lemniscal system
Tickling and itching	Sensations caused by vibrations
Pain	Sensations of friction against the skin
Diffuse sensations of tact or pressure	Sensation of body position in space
Sexual sensations	Sensations of fine touch
Thermal sensations	

somatosensory area, at the thalamus level. This path is called the dorsal column system (or lemniscal system) and is located in the posterior part of the spinal cord. Table C.2 indicates which pathway (spinothalamic or lemniscal) is used by different sensations for reaching the brain.

C.3   Methods for Studying Brain

Even though this information goes slightly beyond the scope of this book, it is worth recalling the main techniques used to ascertain the relationships between brain structures and different sensory, perceptual, or cognitive functions.

As early as the nineteenth century, links were established between brain damage or removal of certain groups of neurons and affected functions. It is now possible to create lesions, in animals, to test hypotheses about the role of the specific brain areas that are damaged. Similarly, since the mid-twentieth century, neurophysiology techniques were developed for implanting microelectrodes to collect the activity of single neurons and their role in sensory physiology.

Nowadays, there are many techniques that allow to draw a general picture, or an image, of brain activity. Generally, they allow or have a fair idea of the location of a structure involved in the function tested or a fair idea regarding when a cerebral contribution occurs. Thus, for nearly 50 years, surface electrodes (on the scalp) were used to measure electrical activity in the brain. This method, called electroencephalography (EEG), reflects the average activity of certain parts of the brain and how this activity changes over a given period. A particular form of this EEG activity is called evoked potentials. These analyses allow to linking quite precisely in time a change in electrical activity and the presentation of sensory stimuli. The electrical activity of the brain also produces small magnetic fields. Thus, a relatively new technique, called magnetoencephalography (MEG), captures the magnetic activity and offers, in addition to a good temporal resolution as is the case for EEG, better spatial resolution since magnetic activity is less vulnerable than the electrical activity captured by the surface electrodes to the distortions caused, for example, by the skull.

Among the tools offered by technology to researchers in neuroscience, there is positron emission tomography. This technique, available for 50 years, measures the metabolic activity of the brain using radioactive tracers. It allows to locate some functions, but offers poor temporal resolution. The 1990s saw the emergence of a technique called functional magnetic resonance imaging. This technique, which does not require the use of radioactive substances, is based on the metabolic changes within the brain. It is thus possible to link the blood flow, as well as the amount of oxygen required by neurons, with some perceptual or cognitive activity. This technique allows a very high spatial resolution.

We can now count on neuromodulation techniques to better understand the properties of the brain. One of these techniques, the transcranial magnetic stimulation, has been available since the mid-1990s. This is a technique where one can create for a short time, with small magnetic pulses, a change in brain activity. One can, for example, create a temporary inability to use a small area of the brain and see how it affects a perceptual or cognitive ability. Even more recently, it has become possible to use *transcranial direct-current stimulation* (tDCS), a noninvasive technique where the application of a small current passes through two electrodes: anode and cathode. The efficacy of tDCS depends on the position of the electrode and the intensity of the current. The anodal stimulation would increase synaptic transmission while cathodal stimulation would inhibit it.

References

Bagot, J.-D. (1996). *Information, sensation et perception*. Paris: Armand Colin.

Bausenhart, K. M., Rolke, B., & Ulrich, R. (2008). Temporal preparation improves temporal resolution: Evidence from constant foreperiods. *Perception & Psychophysics, 70,* 1504–1514.

Biederman, I. (1987). Recognition-by-components: A theory of human image understanding. *Psychological Review, 94,* 115–147.

Bonnet, C. (1986). *Manuel pratique de psychophysique*. Paris: Armand Colin.

Bowmaker, J. K., & Dartnell, H. J. A. (1980). Visual pigments of rods and cones in a human retina. *Journal of Physiology, 298,* 501–511.

Bowmaker, J. K., Dartnell, H. J. A., & Mollon, J. D. (1980). Microspectrophotometric demonstration of four classes of photoreceptor in an old world primate, *Macaca fascicularis*. *Journal of Physiology, 298,* 131–143.

Bregman, A. S. (1990). *Auditory scene analysis (The perceptual organization of sound)*. Cambridge, MA: MIT Press.

Broadbent, D. (1958). *Perception and communication*. London: Pergamon Press.

Bruce, V., Green, P. R., & Georgeson, M. A. (1996). *Visual perception (physiology, psychology, and ecology)* (3rd ed.). Sussex, England: Psychology Press.

Brungart, D. S., Durlach, N. I., & Rabinowitz, W. M. (1999). Auditory localization of nearby sources. II. Localization of a broadband source. *Journal of the Acoustical Society of America, 106,* 1956–1968.

Butler, R. A., Levy, E. T., & Neff, W. D. (1980). Apparent distance of sounds recorded in echoic and anechoic chambers. *Journal of Experimental Psychology: Human Perception and Performance, 6,* 745–750.

Calvert, G., Spence, C., & Stein, B. E. (2004). *The handbook of multisensory processes*. Cambridge, MA: MIT Press.

Campbell, F. W., & Robson, J. G. (1968). Application of Fourier analysis to the visibility of gratings. *Journal of Physiology, 197,* 551–566.

Chaudhuri, A. (2011). *Fundamentals of sensory perception*. New York: Oxford University Press.

Cherry, C. (1953). Some experiments on the recognition of speech with one or two ears. *Journal of the Acoustical Society of America, 25,* 975–979.

Coren, S., & Girgus, J. S. (1978). *Seeing is deceiving: The psychology of visual illusions*. Hillsdale, NJ: Lawrence Erlbaum Associates.

Coren, S., Girgus, J. S., Ehrlichman, H., & Hakstian, A. R. (1976). An empirical taxonomy of visual illusions. *Perception and Psychophysics, 20,* 129–137.

Coren, S., Ward, L. M., & Enns, J. (2004). *Sensation and perception* (6th ed.). Toronto, Ontario, Canada: HBJ.

Cowan, N. (1995). *Attention and memory: An integrated framework*. New York: Oxford University Press.

Dalton, P., & Fraenkel, N. (2012). Gorillas we have missed: Sustained inattentional deafness for dynamic events. *Cognition, 124*, 367–372.

Delorme, A. (1982). *Psychologie de la perception*. Montréal, Québec, Canada: Études Vivantes.

Delorme, A., & Flückiger, M. (2003). *Perception et réalité (Une introduction à la psychologie des perceptions)*. Boucherville, Québec, Canada: Gaëtan Morin.

Desrochers, A. (1990). *Langage et processus cognitifs*. Manuel pour l'éducation à distance. Université Laurentienne, Sudbury, Ontario, Canada.

Deutsch, D. (2010, July). The paradox of pitch circularity. *Acoustics Today*, 8–15.

Deutsch, J. A., & Deutsch, D. (1963). Attention: Some theoretical considerations. *Psychological Review, 70*, 80–90.

DeValois, R. L., Abramovet, J., & Jacobs, G. H. (1966). Analysis of response patterns of LGN cells. *Journal of Optical Society of America, 56*, 966–977.

DeValois, R. L., & DeValois, K. K. (1975). Neural coding of color. In E. C. Carterette and M. P. Friedman (Eds.), *Handbook of perception* (Vol. 5, pp. 117–166). New York: Academic.

DeValois, R. L., & DeValois, K. K. (1988). *Spatial vision (Oxford Psychology Series)*. New York: Oxford University Press.

Di Lollo, V., & Bischof, W. F. (1995). The inverse intensity effect in duration of visible persistence. *Psychological Bulletin, 118*, 223–237.

Diehl, R. L., Lotto, A. J., & Holt, L. L. (2004). Speech perception. *Annual Review of Psychology, 55*, 149–179.

Dowling, J. E., & Boycott, B. B. (1966). Organization of the primate retina: Electron microscopy. *Proceedings of the Royal Society of London. Series B: Biological Sciences, 166*, 80–111.

Dux, P. E., & Marois, R. (2009). The attentional blink: A review of data and theory. *Attention, Perception, & Psychophysics, 71*, 1683–1700.

Eimas, P. D., & Corbit, J. D. (1973). Selective adaptation of linguistic feature detectors. *Cognitive Psychology, 4*, 99–109.

Eisler, H. (1976). Experiments on subjective duration 1878-1975: A collection of power function exponents. *Psychological Bulletin, 83*, 185–200.

Epstein, W. (Ed.). (1977). *Perceptual stability and constancy: Mechanisms and processes*. New York: Wiley.

Fechner, G. (1966). *Elements of psychophysics* (H. E. Adler, D. H. Howes & E. G. Boring, Trans.). New York: Holt, Rinehart & Winston. (Original work published 1860)

Fletcher, H., & Munson, W. A. (1933). Loudness, its definition, measurement and calculation. *Journal of the Acoustical Society of America, 6*, 82–108.

Foley, H. J., & Matlin, M. W. (2010). *Sensation and perception* (5th ed.). Toronto, Ontario, Canada: Allyn and Bacon.

Galantucci, B., Fowler, C. A., & Turvey, M. T. (2006). The motor theory of speech perception reviewed. *Psychonomic Bulletin & Review, 13*, 361–377.

Gazzaniga, M. S., Ivry, R. B., & Mangun, G. R. (2009). *Cognitive neuroscience—The biology of the mind* (3rd ed.). New York: Norton.

Gescheider, G. A. (1997). *Psychophysics: Method, theory, and applications* (3rd ed.). Hillsdale, NJ: Lawrence Erlbaum.

Gibson, J. J. (1966). *The senses considered as perceptual systems*. Boston: Houghton Mifflin.

Gibson, J. J. (1979). *The ecological approach to visual perception*. Boston: Houghton Mifflin.

Gibson, E. J., Schapiro, F., & Yonas, A. (1968). Confusion matrices for graphic patterns obtained with a latency measure. *The analysis of reading skill: A program of basic and applied research*. (Final Report, Project No. 5–1213). Ithaca, NY: Cornell University and U.S. Office of Education.

Ginsburg, A. P., Evans, D. W., Sekuler, R., & Harp, S. A. (1982). Contrast sensitivity predicts performance in aircraft simulators. *American Journal of Optometry and Physiological Optics, 59*, 105–109.

Girgus, J. S., & Coren, S. (1975). Depth cues and constancy scaling in the horizontal-vertical illusion: The bisection error. *Canadian Journal of Psychology, 29*, 59–65.

Goldstein, E. B. (2010). *Sensation and perception* (8th ed.). Belmont, CA: Wadsworth.

Gray, J. A., & Wedderburn, A. I. (1960). Grouping strategies with simultaneous stimuli. *Quarterly Journal of Experimental Psychology, 12*, 180–184.

Gregory, R. L. (1997). Knowledge in perception and illusion. *Philosophical Transactions of the Royal Society of London, 352*, 1121–1128.

Grondin, S. (2001). From physical time to the first and second moments of psychological time. *Psychological Bulletin, 127*, 22–44.

Grondin, S. (2008). Methods for studying psychological time. In S. Grondin (Ed.), *Psychology of time* (pp. 51–74). Bingley, England: Emerald Group.

Grondin, S. (2010). Timing and time perception: A review of recent behavioral and neuroscience findings and theoretical directions. *Attention, Perception, & Psychophysics, 72*, 561–582.

Grondin, S. (2012). Violation of the scalar property for time perception between 1 and 2 seconds: Evidence from interval discrimination, reproduction, and categorization. *Journal of Experimental Psychology: Human Perception and Performance, 38*, 880–890.

Grondin, S., & Killeen, P. R. (2009). Tracking time with song and count: Different Weber functions for musicians and non-musicians. *Attention, Perception, & Psychophysics, 71*, 1649–1654.

Grondin, S., & Laflamme, V. (2015). Stevens's law for time: A direct comparison of prospective and retrospective judgments. *Attention, Perception, & Psychophysics, 77*, 1044–1051.

Grondin, S., & Laforest, M. (2004). Discriminating slow tempo variations in a musical context. *Acoustical Science & Technology, 25*, 159–162.

Gulick, W. L., Gescheider, G. A., & Frisina, R. D. (1989). *Hearing: Physiological acoustics, neural coding, and psychophysics*. New York: Oxford University Press.

Harmon, L. D., & Julesz, B. (1973). Masking in visual recognition: Effects of two-dimensional filtered noise. *Science, 180*, 1194–1197.

Hartline, H. K. (1940). The receptive fields of optic nerve fibers. *American Journal of Physiology, 130*, 690–699.

Hartline, H. K., & Ratliff, F. (1957). Inhibitory interaction of receptor units in the eye of limulus. *Journal of General Physiology, 40*, 357–376.

Hartmann, W. M. (1996). Pitch, periodicity, and auditory organization. *Journal of the Acoustical Society of America, 100*, 3491–3502.

Hellström, Å. (1985). The time-order error and its relatives: Mirrors of cognitive processes in comparing. *Psychological Bulletin, 97*, 35–61.

Hershenson, M. (Ed.). (1989). *The moon illusion*. Hillsdale, NJ: Lawrence Erlbaum.

Holway, A. H., & Boring, E. G. (1941). Determinants of apparent visual size with distance variant. *American Journal of Psychology, 54*, 21–37.

Honegger, M. (Ed.). (1976). *Science de la musique* (Vol. 1–2). Paris: Bordas.

Hubel, D. H., & Wiesel, T. N. (1959). Receptive fields of single neurones in the cat's striate cortex. *Journal of Physiology, 148*, 574–591.

Hubel, D. H., & Wiesel, T. N. (1962). Receptive fields, binocular interaction and functional architecture in the cat's visual cortex. *Journal of Physiology, 160*, 106–154.

Hubel, D. H., & Wiesel, T. N. (1968). Receptive fields, binocular interaction, and functional architecture in monkey striate cortex. *Journal of Physiology, 168*, 215–243.

Jesse, A., & Massaro, D. W. (2010). Seeing a singer helps comprehension of the song's lyrics. *Psychonomic Bulletin & Review, 17*, 323–328.

Johnston, W. A., & Dark, V. J. (1986). Selective attention. *Annual Review of Psychology, 37*, 43–75.

Kaufman, L., & Rock, I. (1962). The moon illusion. *Scientific American, 207*, 120–132.

Kilpatrick, F. P., & Ittelson, W. H. (1953). The size-distance invariance hypothesis. *Psychological Review, 60*, 223–231.

Klein, R. M. (2000). Inhibition of return. *Trends in Cognitive Sciences, 4*, 138–147.

Kluender, K. L., Diehl, R. L., & Killeen, P. R. (1987). Japanese quail can learn phonetic categories. *Science, 237*, 1195–1197.

Kuffler, S. W. (1953). Discharge patterns and functional organization of mammalian retina. *Journal of Neurophysiology, 16*, 37–68.

Kuroda, T., Nakajima, Y., Tsunashima, S., & Yasutake, T. (2009). Effects of spectra and sound pressure levels on the occurrence of the gap transfer illusion. *Perception, 38*, 411–428.

Larsen, E., Iyer, N., Lansing, C. R., & Feng, A. S. (2008). On the minimum audible difference in direct-to-reverberant energy ratio. *Journal of the Acoustical Society of America, 124*, 450–461.

Le Petit Larousse illustré 2011 – Dictionary (2010). Paris: Larousse.

Livingstone, M. S., & Hubel, D. H. (1987). Psychophysical evidence for separate channels for the perception of form, color, movement, and depth. *Journal of Neuroscience, 7*, 3416–3468.

Loftus, G. R., & Irwin, D. E. (1998). On the relations among different measures of visible and informational persistence. *Cognitive Psychology, 35*, 135–199.

Lortie, J.-Y., & Parent, G. (1989). *Psychologie de la perception—Notes de cours*. Sainte-Foy, Quebec, Canada: Université Laval.

Macdonald, J. S. P., & Lavie, N. (2011). Visual perceptual load induces inattentional deafness. *Attention, Perception, & Psychophysics, 73*, 1780–1789.

Mack, A., & Rock, I. (1998). *Inattentional blindness*. Cambridge, MA: MIT Press.

MacLeod, C. M. (1991). Half a century of research on the Stroop effect: An integrative review. *Psychological Bulletin, 109*, 163–203.

Macmillan, N. A., & Creelman, C. D. (1991). *Detection theory: A user's guide*. New York: Cambridge University Press.

Marr, D. (1982). *Vision: A computational investigation into the human representation and processing of visual information*. New York: Freeman.

Marr, D., & Nishihara, H. K. (1978). Representation and recognition of the spatial organization of three-dimensional shapes. *Proceedings of the Royal Society of London B, 200*, 269–294.

Martensa, S., & Wybleb, B. (2010). The attentional blink: Past, present, and future of a blind spot in perceptual awareness. *Neuroscience and Biobehavioral Reviews, 34*, 947–957.

McCollough, C. (1965). Adaptation of edge-detectors in the human visual system. *Science, 149*, 1115–1116.

McGurk, H., & MacDonald, J. (1976). Hearing lips and seeing voices. *Nature, 264*, 746–748.

Michael, C. R. (1978). Color vision mechanisms in monkey striate cortex: Dual-opponent cells with concentric receptive fields. *Journal of Neurophysiology, 41*, 572–588.

Miller, G. A. (1947). The masking of speech. *Psychological Bulletin, 44*, 105–129.

Miller, G. A., & Licklider, J. C. R. (1950). The intelligibility of interrupted speech. *Journal of the Acoustical Society of America, 22*, 167–173.

Musicant, A. D., & Butler, R. A. (1984). The influence of pinnae-based spectral cues on sound localization. *Journal of the Acoustical Society of America, 75*, 1195–1200.

Nakajima, Y., Sasaki, T., Kanafuka, K., Miyamoto, A., Remijn, G., & ten Hoopen, G. (2000). Illusory recouplings of onsets and terminations of glide tone components. *Perception and Psychophysics, 62*, 1413–1425.

Neisser, U. (1964). Visual search. *Scientific American, 210*(6), 94–102.

Niemi, P., & Näätänen, R. (1981). Foreperiod and simple reaction time. *Psychological Bulletin, 89*, 133–162.

Nisly, S. J., & Wasserman, G. S. (1989). Intensity dependence of perceived duration: Data, theories, and neural integration. *Psychological Bulletin, 106*, 483–496.

Palmer, S. E. (1992). Common regions: A new principle of perceptual grouping. *Cognitive Psychology, 24*, 436–447.

Patel, A. D. (2008). *Music, language, and the brain*. New York: Oxford University Press.

Penrose, L. S., & Penrose, R. (1958). Impossible objects: A special type of visual illusion. *British Journal of Psychology, 49*, 31–33.

Peretz, I., & Hyde, K. L. (2003). What is specific to music processing? Insights from congenital amusia. *Trends in Cognitive Sciences, 7*, 362–367.

Piaget, J. (1961). *Les mécanismes perceptifs*. Paris: PUF.

Posner, M. I. (1978). *Chronometric exploration of mind*. Hillsdale: Erlbaum.

Posner, M. I., & Cohen, Y. (1984). Components of visual orienting. In H. Bouma & D. Bouwhuis (Eds.), *Attention & performance X* (pp. 531–556). Hillsdale, NJ: Erlbaum.

Prinzmetal, W., & Gettleman, L. (1993). Vertical-horizontal illusion: One eye is better than two. *Perception & Psychophysics, 53*, 81–88.

Rafal, R. D., Calabresi, P. A., Brennan, C. W., & Sciolto, T. K. (1989). Saccade preparation inhibits reorienting to recently attended locations. *Journal of Experimental Psychology: Human Perception and Performance, 15*, 673–685.

Reed, S. K. (1982). *Cognition: Theory and applications.* Monterrey, CA: Brooks/Cole.

Rensink, R. A. (2002). Change detection. *Annual Review of Psychology, 53*, 245–277.

Rensink, R. A., O'Regan, J. K., & Clark, J. J. (1997). To see or not to see: The need for attention to perceive changes in scenes. *Psychological Science, 8*, 368–373.

Rock, I., & Kaufman, L. (1962). The moon illusion, II: The moon's apparent size is a function of the presence or absence of terrain. *Science, 136*, 1023–1031.

Rosenzweig, M. R., Leiman, A. L., & Breedlove, S. M. (1998). *Psychobiologie.* New York: Random House.

Ross, H., & Plug, C. (2002). *The mystery of the moon illusion: Exploring size perception.* Oxford, England: Oxford University Press.

Sasaki, T. (1980). Sound restoration and temporal localization of noise in speech and music sounds. *Tohoku Psychologica Folia, 39*, 79–88.

Schiffman, H. R. (2001). *Sensation and perception: An integrated approach* (5th ed.). New York: Wiley.

Sekuler, R., & Blake, R. (1990). *Perception* (2nd ed.). Toronto, Ontario, Canada: McGraw-Hill.

Selfridge, O. G. (1959). Pandemonium: A paradigm of learning. In D. V. Blake & A. M. Uttley (Eds.), *The mechanization of thought processes* (pp. 523–526). London: HM Stationery Office.

Shen, Y. (2013). Comparing adaptive procedures for estimating the psychometric function for an auditory gap detection task. *Attention, Perception and Psychophysics, 75*, 771–780.

Shen, Y., & Richards, V. M. (2012). A maximum-likelihood procedure for estimating psychometric functions: Thresholds, slopes, and lapses of attention. *Journal of Acoustical Society of America, 132*, 957–967.

Shepard, R. N. (1964). Circularity in judgments of relative pitch. *Journal of the Acoustical Society of America, 36*, 2346–2353.

Shepard, R. N. (1990). *Mind sight.* New York: Freeman.

Simons, D. J., & Chabris, C. F. (1999). Gorillas in our midst: Sustained inattentional blindness for dynamic events. *Perception, 28*, 1059–1074.

Snyder, J. S., & Alain, C. (2007). Toward a neurophysiology theory of auditory stream segregation. *Psychological Bulletin, 133*, 780–799.

Sperling, G. (1960). The information available in brief visual presentations. *Psychological Monographs, 74*, 1–29.

Stevens, S. S. (1961). The psychophysics of sensory functions. In A. W. Rosenblith (Ed.), *Sensory communication* (pp. 1–33). Cambridge, MA: MIT Press.

Stevens, S. S. (1975). *Psychophysics: Introduction to its perceptual, neural and social prospects.* New York: Wiley.

Strayer, D. L., & Johnston, W. A. (2001). Driven to distraction: Dual-task studies of simulated driving and conversing on a cellular phone. *Psychological Science, 12*, 462–466.

Stroop, J. R. (1935). Studies of interference in serial verbal reactions. *Journal of Experimental Psychology, 18*, 643–662.

Thompson, W. F., Russo, R. A., & Livingstone, S. (2010). Facial expressions of pitch structure in music performance. *Psychonomic Bulletin & Review, 17*, 317–322.

Treisman, A. M. (1960). Contextual cues in selective listening. *Quarterly Journal of Experimental Psychology, 12*, 242–248.

Treisman, A. M. (1996). The binding problem. *Current Opinion in Neurobiology, 6*, 171–178.

Treisman, A. M., & Gelade, G. (1980). A feature-integration theory of attention. *Cognitive Psychology, 12*, 97–136.

Treisman, A. M., & Schmidt, H. (1982). Illusory conjunctions in the perception of objects. *Cognitive Psychology, 14*, 107–141.

Tsao, D. Y., & Livingstone, M. S. (2008). Mechanisms of face perception. *Annual Review of Neuroscience, 31*, 411–437.

Tsunada, J., Lee, J. H., & Cohen, Y. E. (2011). Representation of speech categories in the primate auditory cortex. *Journal of Neurophysiology, 105*, 2634–2646.

van Noorden, L. P. A. S. (1975). *Temporal coherence in the perception of tone sequences.* Unpublished doctoral dissertation. Eindhoven University of Technology, Eindhoven, Netherlands.

Warren, R. M. (1970). Perceptual restoration of missing speech sounds. *Science, 167*, 392–393.

Weiskrantz, L. (1986). *Blindsight: A case study and implications.* Oxford, England: Oxford University Press.

Werner, H. (1935). Studies on contour: I. Quantitative analysis. *American Journal of Psychology, 47*, 40–64.

Wever, E. G., & Bray, C. W. (1937). The perception of low tones and the resonance-volley theory. *Journal of Psychology, 3*, 101–114.

Wightman, F. L., & Kistler, D. J. (1992). The dominant role of low-frequency interaural time differences in sound localization. *Journal of the Acoustical Society of America, 91*, 648–1661.

Wolfe, J. M., & Horowitz, T. S. (2004). What attributes guide the deployment of visual attention and how do they do it? *Nature Reviews Neuroscience, 5*, 1–7.

Wolfe, J. M., Kluender, K. R., Levi, D. M., Bartoshuk, L. M., Herz, R. S., Klatzky, R. L., et al. (2006). *Sensation and perception.* Sunderland, MA: Sinauer.

Yost, W. A. (2009). Pitch perception. *Attention, Perception and Psychophysics, 71*, 1701–1716.

Index

A

Absolute threshold, 1
Aerial perspective, 109
Affordance, 115
After image, 78
Agnosia, 101
Amusia, 46
Aqueous humor, 54
Assimilation effects, 78
Astigmatism, 63
Attention process, 124–125
Auditory adaptation, 32
Auditory continuity, 38
Auditory selectivity, 130–133

B

Balint syndrome, 135
Binocular convergence, 104
Bipolar cells, 56, 57
Blindnesses, 124–125
Blindsight, 135
Blind spot, 55
Boring, 113, 114
Brightness constancy, 111

C

Cataract, 64
Central deafness, 32
Cerumen, 25
Chroma, 43
Chromatic effects, 76–80
Cochlea, 27–28
Color constancy, 80, 111

Color perception
    chromatic effects, 76–80
    clinical aspects, 80–81
    color mixtures
        addition and subtraction, 72–74
        primary colors, 71
    color vision, 74–76
    light intensity, 68
    perceptual dimensions, 70
    wavelength and spectral composition, 68–70
Commission internationale de l'éclairage
        (CIE), 71
Common region, 93
Complex sound wave, 20–22
Computational theory, 99–100
Connectedness, 93
Contrast sensitivity function (CSF), 97–98
Cross disparity, 105

D

Delboeuf illusions, 120
Depth perception
    constancy
        Gibson's perspective, 114–115
        interpretations and investigations,
            112–114
        types, 111
    cues, 103
        binocular convergence, 104
        monocular, 106–111
        retinal disparity, 105
    illusions
        classification, 115–118
        moon, 118–122

Dichromatism, 80
Difference threshold, 6
Doppler effect, 42

E
Ecological position, 114
Emmert's law, 112
Equalization effects, 78
Equal-loudness contours, 23
Eustachian tube, 26
Eye
    clinical aspects, 63–65
    eyeball, 53–55
    receptive fields, 57–59
    retina, 55–57
    visual cortex, 60–61
    visual pathways, 61–63

F
Facilitation effect, 126
Fechner, Gustav, 1
Form perception, 87, 93
    agnosia, 101
    computational approach, 99–100
    edges and subjective contours, 84–85
    factors, 87–89
    Gestalt (see Gestalt)
    lateral inhibition, 85–86
    Mach bands, 86–87
    multiple spatial channels (see Multiple
        spatial channels theory)
    structural model, 100–101
    templates/characteristics, 98–99
Frequency theory, 29–30

G
Ganglion cells, 58, 59
Ganzfeld, 83
Gap transfer, 36–39
Gestalt, 89
    figure/ground distinction, 90–92
    laws, 92
    perceptual grouping, 92–93
Gibson's perspective, 114–115
Glaucoma, 65
Good continuation, 93

H
Hallucinations, 115
Head transfer function, 41
Hearing

central mechanisms, 28
clinical aspects, 32–33
cochlea, 27–28
complex sound wave, 20–22
gap transfer, 36–39
illusion of continuity, 36–39
music
    subjective experience, 45–46
    technical description, 43–45
outer, middle, and inner ear, 25–26
sound wave (see Sound wave)
speech
    intermodality, 49–50
    linguistic description, 46–47
    technical analysis, 48–49
    theoretical perspectives, 49–50
streaming, 36
theory
    frequency, 29–30
    location, 30–31
Hering, Ewald, 74, 75
Holway, 113, 114
Horizontal-vertical illusion, 120
Hydrodynamic movement, 30
Hypermetropia, 63

I
Illuminance, 68
Illusions
    classification, 115–118
    of continuity, 36–39
    moon, 118–122
Incident light, 68
Inclusion, 92
Inhibition of return, 126
Interaural time difference, 40
Internal articulation, 92
Interposition, 106

J
Just noticeable difference (JND), 6

L
Lateral geniculate nucleus (LGN), 59
Lateral inhibition, 85–86
Law of closure, 93
Law of common fate, 93
Law of good form, 93
Law of pragnanz, 93
Law of proximity, 92
Law of similarity, 92
Light intensity, 68

Linear perspective, 106
Luminance, 68

M
Mach bands, 86–88
Magnitude estimation, 14
McCollough effect, 79
Metathetic continuum, 16
Mondegreen, 51
Monochromatism, 81
Morphemes, 47
Motion parallax, 109
Müller-Lyer illusion, 116, 117
Multiple spatial channels theory
    concepts, 93–96
    CSF, 97–98
Myopia, 63

N
Nonspectral colors, 74
Nystagmus, 65

O
Occlusion, 106
Oppel-Kundt illusion, 120
Optic chiasm, 63
Organ of Corti, 27
Orientation, 94

P
Pandemonium theory, 99
Parameter estimation by sequential testing
    (PEST), 13
Parvotemporal pathway, 62
Perception, 124, 128
    attention process (*see* Attention process)
    clinical aspects, 135
    selectivity (*see* Selectivity)
    spatial preparation, 125–127
    temporal preparation, 127–128
    visual search, 133–134
Perceptive deafness, 32
Perfect pitch, 46
Phase difference, 40
Phase locking, 29
Phonemes, 46, 47
Photosensitive pigments, 56
Point of subjective equality (PSE), 6
Ponzo illusion, 117, 118
Presbycusis, 32

Presbyopia, 63
Prosopagnosia, 101
Prothetic continuum, 15
Psychometric function, 3
Psychophysical law, 14
Psychophysics
    detection, 1–2
        absolute threshold and constant stimuli,
            2–3
        SDT (*see* Signal detection theory (SDT))
    discrimination
        difference threshold and constant
            stimuli, 6–8
        Weber's law, 8–9
    methods for thresholds
        adaptive methods, 12–13
        method of adjustment, 9–10
        method of limits, 10–12
    scaling, 13–15

R
Receptive fields, 57–59
Relative brightness, 108
Relative height, 107
Relative sharpness, 109
Retina, 55–57
Retinal disparity, 105

S
Sander's illusion, 116
Sclera, 54
Scotoma, 65
Selectivity
    auditory, 130–133
    visual, 128–130
Sensorineural deafness, 32
Shape constancy, 111
Shepard's auditory illusion, 40
Signal detection theory (SDT)
    concepts, 3–5
    units of measurement, 5–6
Simultaneous contrast, 77
Size constancy, 111
Size-distance invariance principle, 112
Sound pressure level (SPL), 19
Sound wave
    amplitude, 19–20
    frequency and phase, 17–19
    location of direction, 40–41
    location of distance, 41–42
    subjective characteristics, 23–24
Spatial frequency, 94

Spatial preparation, 125–127
Speed constancy, 111
Sperling, George, 129
Stevens's law, 14–15
Stimulus onset asynchrony (SOA), 126
Strabismus, 65
Stroop effect, 132
Structural model, 100–101
Surroundedness, 92

T
Tectopulvinar pathway, 62
Template matching model, 99
Temporal preparation, 127–128
Titchener illusions, 120
Trichromatic theory, 74–76
Trichromatism, 80

U
Unconscious inference, 112
Uncrossed disparity, 105

V
Ventral pathway, 62
Ventriloquism, 42
Visual perception
    clinical aspects, 63–65
    eyeball, 53–55
    receptive fields, 57–59
    retina, 55–57
    visual cortex, 60–61
    visual pathways, 61–63
Visual search, 133–134
Visual selectivity, 128–130
Vitreous humor, 54
Voice onset time, 50
Volley principle, 29, 30

W
Weber's law, 8–9

Y
Young-Helmholtz, 74, 75

CPI Antony Rowe
Eastbourne, UK
March 29, 2019